Successful Writing

UPPER-INTERMEDIATE

Virginia Evans

Express Publishing

Introduction

To the Teacher

Successful Writing Upper-Intermediate consists of 19 units which cover all types of composition writing (descriptions, narratives, transactional and other types of letters, argumentative essays, articles, reviews) required at FCE level. Each unit starts with a lead-in listening activity through which the basic plan for the type of writing the unit deals with is introduced. This also serves as a brainstorming activity, giving the teacher the chance to elicit useful language and ideas on the topic under discussion. Detailed theory and plans are provided to be used as a reference by students. A variety of models in which the theory is applied are followed by exercises to improve students' writing skills, focusing on register and style. The exercises are graded, leading to the acquisition of those skills needed for students to be able to write successfully at FCE level. Topic identification, revision boxes and study check sections reinforce students' knowledge and remind them of the structures previously presented, thus helping them revise the writing areas covered in the book. The Teacher's Book provides answers to the exercises, model plans, transcripts of the listening exercises and useful teaching tips. At the back of the Teacher's Book are marked model compositions to help teachers mark students' compositions. The book is accompanied by a cassette with all the listening exercises.

The units can either be presented in the order they appear in the book or teachers can select the unit they want to present according to their own judgement and their students' needs. The course can be covered in approximately 30 one-hour lessons.

Brainstorming Technique

The brainstorming technique can be used in all the units presented in this book. The technique may be applied each time the students come across a new topic, whether in a model or a writing assignment.

The technique is used as follows: the teacher invites students to say as many words or ideas as possible related to the topic and writes them on the board. The teacher may choose to guide the students further by having them link or categorise related terms. Students then proceed to do the exercise on their own.

This technique aims to stimulate students' knowledge about the topic, thus drawing together ideas and vocabulary necessary for writing a successful composition.

e.g. Discuss the advantages and disadvantages of living in the country.
Brainstorming: *quiet, noisy, no flats, nice gardens, lots of trees, not many cars, few hospitals, no stress, few schools, not many cinemas, no pollution, healthy surroundings,* etc.

e.g. Describe your best friend.
Brainstorming. T writes the following key words on the board and asks Ss to give him/her as many words as possible related to each key word

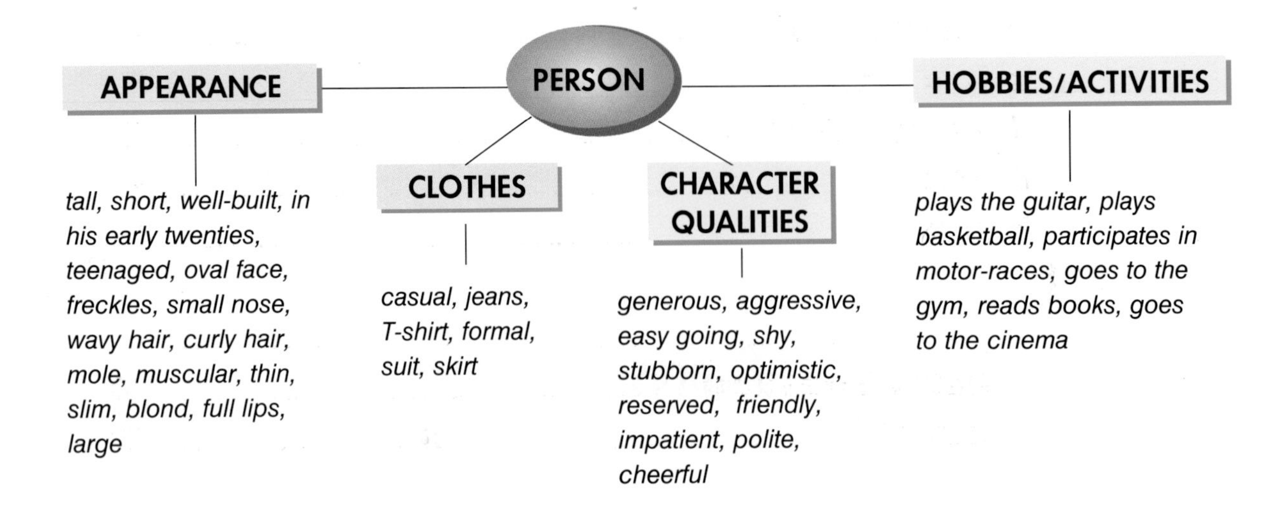

Contents

UNIT 1 Describing People

1 **Read the following table, then listen to the cassette and tick the information mentioned. Finally, use the table and the photograph to describe Paul.**

Height	quite tall ☐	rather short ☐		
Build	well-built ☐	thin ☐		muscular ☐
Age	early twenties ☐	mid thirties ☐		teenaged ☐
Facial Features	oval face ☐	high cheekbones ☐	blue eyes ☐	mole ☐
Hair	curly ☐	short brown ☐	wavy ☐	
Clothes	casual ☐	formal ☐		
Personality	good-humoured ☐	imaginative ☐	vain ☐	short-tempered ☐
Activities/Hobbies	going to discos ☐	watching old films ☐	cooking ☐	

A descriptive composition about a person should consist of:

a) an **introduction** where you give some brief information about the person (his/her name, time or place you met/saw him/her, how you heard about him/her);

b) a **main body** where you describe physical appearance, personality characteristics and hobbies/interests/everyday activities in separate paragraphs; and

c) a **conclusion** which includes your comments and/or feelings about the person.

Such descriptions can be found in articles, letters, witness statements, novels, etc.

Points to consider

- Each paragraph starts with a topic sentence which introduces the subject of the paragraph. A variety of linking words should be used to connect ideas.
- To describe physical appearance, details should be given as follows: **height/build, age, facial features, hair, clothes,** moving from the most general aspects to the more specific details. *e.g. John is a tall, slim man in his mid forties. He has a thin face, blue eyes and a large nose. His short hair is greying at the temples. He is usually casually dressed.*
- To describe character and behaviour you can support your description with examples. *e.g. Sally is very sociable. She loves going to parties and dances.* If you want to mention any negative qualities, use mild language (tends to, seems to, is rather, can occasionally be, etc.). *e.g.* Instead of saying *Sally is arrogant.*, it is better to say *Sally tends to be rather arrogant.*
- Variety in the use of adjectives will make your description more interesting. *e.g. good-natured, well-behaved, gorgeous, etc.*
- Present tenses can be used to describe someone connected to the present, *e.g. someone you see every day.* Past tenses can be used to describe someone related to the past, *e.g. someone who is no longer alive, someone whom you won't meet again ... etc.*

Introduction

Paragraph 1

name of the person; time you met/saw him/her

Main Body

Paragraph 2

physical appearance

Paragraph 3

personality characteristics and justification

Paragraph 4

hobbies, interests or any activities he/she takes part in

Conclusion

Final Paragraph

comments & feelings about the person

2 **Read the model composition and write down the topic of each paragraph. Find the topic sentences for each paragraph and try to replace them with other similar ones. Then underline the adjectives which describe physical appearance and circle the ones which describe personality.**

"My Next-door Neighbour"

Mavis, neighbour for six years

Mavis has been my neighbour for six years. I first met her when she knocked on my door and asked for a spade because she hadn't yet unpacked hers. She had only moved in two days before.

Physically, Mavis looks younger than most other women in their late sixties. She is of average height, neither fat nor thin. Her plump round face is framed by a mass of wavy white hair and her sparkling blue eyes show her humour and friendliness. She prefers wearing casual, comfortable clothes. I don't think I have ever seen her in a perfectly ironed suit.

As for her personality, Mavis's most striking characteristic is her generosity. My house, as well as most of our neighbours', nearly always has a vase of flowers from her garden in the living room. Mavis is very good- natured and always has time for a chat. She is also patient. She hardly ever gets annoyed about anything, except when children pick her favourite roses and lilies. However, she tends to be quite stubborn – once she has made a decision, nothing can change her mind.

Mavis always seems to be busy doing something. She spends a lot of her time looking after her garden and often participates in local flower shows. When she is not in her garden she is usually off somewhere raising money for one charity or another.

All in all, Mavis is the perfect next-door neighbour. Since the day she moved in, we have grown very close and I am very fond of her, even if I am woken up by the noise of her lawnmower early in the morning!

3 **Fill in the table with words from the list below. Using words from the completed table describe your partner's physical appearance, then write a short paragraph describing the appearance of a relative of yours.**

round, oval, slanted, ginger, of medium height, middle-aged, mole, teenaged, curly, blond, tall, wrinkled, thick, balding, just over six foot, tanned, slim, thin, scar, elderly, muscular, in his teens, well-built, in his mid-forties, overweight, curved, wavy, pale, crooked, freckled, dimples, straight, skinny, beard, shoulder-length, almond-shaped, short, moustache, long-legged, round-shouldered, in his late forties, full

HEIGHT:	
BUILD:	
AGE:	
COMPLEXION:	
FACE:	
HAIR:	
EYES:	
NOSE:	
LIPS:	
SPECIAL FEATURES:	

4 **Match the following adjectives with the nouns below. Some adjectives can be used more than once.**

broad, rosy, clear, bushy, thick, full, upturned, double, hooked, fair, crooked, thin, hollow, deep-set, curly, puffy, clean-shaven, pale, oval, spotty, dark

1	.... eyebrows	6	.... face
2	.... eyes	7	.... lips
3	.... complexion	8	.... cheeks
4	.... nose	9	.... hair
5	.... chin	10	.... shoulders

5 *The man in the photograph is wanted by the police.* **Look at the picture and the text and try to fill in the missing words. Then, listen to the cassette to find out if your answers were correct. Why is there no description of his personality?**

A dangerous prisoner escaped this morning from Spurswall prison. He is believed to be at large in the Waxerton area and police are warning the public not to approach him as he is likely to react violently. Neville Slatter is 6 foot 3 inches tall and quite **1)** .... with **2)** .... shoulders. He is 54 years old and unshaven with a **3)** .... jaw, a large nose and **4)** .... lips. He has **5)** .... untidy brown hair and is bald on top. He also has a **6)** .... on his right cheek. Should you see this man, or if you have knowledge of his whereabouts, please contact your local police station.

Avoid beginning all sentences in the same way as this will make your composition boring. Use a variety of structures, trying to link the sentences together. Instead of writing: *She is a pretty girl. She has an oval face.*, you can write: *She is a pretty girl* **with** *an oval face.*

Look at the examples suggested below:

He has wrinkles. They make him look older.
He has wrinkles **which** *make him look older.*
She is a beautiful woman. She wears designer clothes.
She is a beautiful woman **who** *wears designer clothes.*
She has long hair. She wears her hair in a pony-tail.
She wears her long hair in a pony-tail.
He has a big garden. He grows vegetables in the garden.
He has a big garden **where** *he grows vegetables.*

6 **Rewrite the sentences by linking them together as illustrated in the examples above.**

1 David Keen was well-built. He had fine wrinkles around his eyes. They showed when he laughed.

2 Willy is in his mid twenties. He has an oval face and long curly hair. He ties it back in a pony-tail. He has a big kitchen. He likes to cook for his friends.

3 Helen is dark-skinned. She has beautiful almond-shaped eyes. She dyes her hair. It makes her look younger than she is.

4 Marcy's mother is an attractive woman. She has long blond hair. She wears her hair in a bun.

7 **Use the adjectives listed below to complete the character descriptions.**

honest, reserved, outgoing, frank, tactless, persuasive, trustworthy, fussy

1 Tina is a very ....person. She is capable of convincing you to do almost anything she wants.

2 Sarah can be .... on occasion. She often says things that offend people.

3 Jim is very ....; he always says exactly what he is thinking.

4 Stephanie is one of the most .... people I know; she would never consider doing anything illegal.

5 My little sister is very .... about what she eats; there are very few foods she likes.

6 Anna is a very .... person who hardly ever lets her feelings show.

7 Mark is extremely .... ; when it comes to keeping secrets, he will never tell a soul.

8 Annabel is a(n) .... person who loves meeting people and making new friends.

8 **Decide which adjectives describe positive or negative qualities. Choose any five of them and write sentences justifying each quality, then write a short paragraph describing the character of one of your relatives.**

patient, boring, pessimistic, mean, ambitious, generous, mature, interesting, hostile, immature, friendly, impatient, tactful, good-natured, short-tempered, thick-skinned, easy-going, hard-working, deceitful, fair, shy, helpful, aggressive, reserved, outgoing, polite, cheerful

Positive Qualities	Negative Qualities
patient	*boring*

e.g. My grandmother is very ***patient;*** *she takes time and care with everything she does. etc.*

Sentences can be linked together in a variety of ways. Read the examples and say which words are used to link descriptions of similar qualities and which to join descriptions of opposing qualities.

Similar qualities (both positive or both negative)

e.g. She is kind-hearted. She is cooperative.
She is kind-hearted ***and also*** *cooperative.*
She is kind-hearted ***and*** *cooperative* ***as well.***
She is kind-hearted, ***as well as (being)*** *cooperative.*
In addition to *being kind-hearted, she is* ***also*** *cooperative.*
She is ***both*** *kind-hearted* ***and*** *cooperative.*

Opposing qualities (one positive and one negative)

e.g. He is usually well-behaved. He can be naughty at times.
He is usually well-behaved ***but*** *can be naughty at times.*
He is usually well-behaved; ***in spite of this/nevertheless/however,*** *he can be naughty at times.*
Although/In spite of the fact that *he is usually well-behaved, he can be naughty at times.*

9 **Rewrite the following sentences using linking words/phrases from the table above.**

1 He is humorous. He has a tendency to be immature.
2 He is kind-hearted. He can, on occasion, be absent-minded.
3 She is enthusiastic. She is cooperative.
4 She has a pleasant personality. She can be shy and unsociable.
5 He is well-balanced. He has a sensitive nature.
6 He has a generous disposition. From time to time he can be aggressive.

10 *You are going to hear a conversation between two company executives who are trying to decide which of the two people below should be promoted.*
Read the information and try to fill in the missing adjectives, then listen to find out if your answers were correct.

.... ; he has doubled clientele
.... ; he uses his own judgement to make decisions
.... ; he works well with employees
.... ; he is never late for work

.... ; she has been with the company for many years
.... ; she has difficulty in facing customers
.... ; if her work is criticised, she sometimes bursts into tears

11 Read the following extract and underline the correct linking words/phrases. Then list the positive and negative qualities mentioned. Where do you think this extract is taken from? Why do you think there is no description of physical appearance?

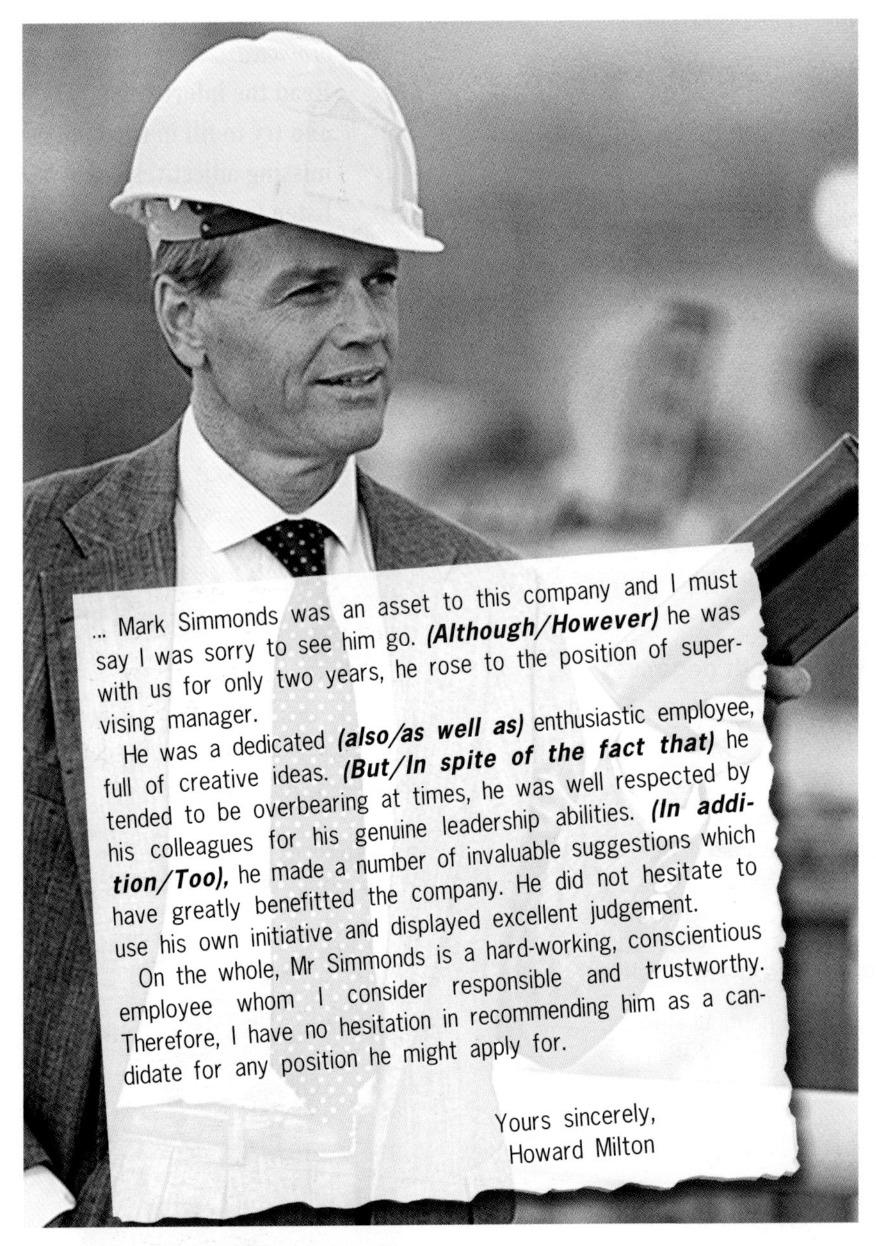

... Mark Simmonds was an asset to this company and I must say I was sorry to see him go. ***(Although/However)*** he was with us for only two years, he rose to the position of supervising manager.

He was a dedicated ***(also/as well as)*** enthusiastic employee, full of creative ideas. ***(But/In spite of the fact that)*** he tended to be overbearing at times, he was well respected by his colleagues for his genuine leadership abilities. ***(In addition/Too),*** he made a number of invaluable suggestions which have greatly benefitted the company. He did not hesitate to use his own initiative and displayed excellent judgement.

On the whole, Mr Simmonds is a hard-working, conscientious employee whom I consider responsible and trustworthy. Therefore, I have no hesitation in recommending him as a candidate for any position he might apply for.

Yours sincerely,
Howard Milton

12 *You used to be the employer of the person whose qualities are listed below. Write a reference for her.* Include a variety of appropriate linking words/phrases, using the model in exercise 11 as a guide. You can start as shown in the example.

reliable, honest, professional, determined, knowledgeable, impatient, cheerful

e.g. Jennifer Grant worked as a teacher for Brighton Primary School for two and a half years.

13 *Pietro's brother, Paolo, is going to study abroad. He will be staying with a couple of Pietro's English friends. His friends are going to meet Paolo at the airport but they haven't seen him since he was little, so Pietro has decided to write them a letter with all the necessary information.* What information should Pietro include in his letter?

14 Listen to the letter Pietro wrote and make notes under each heading. Then, using this information, describe Paolo.

APPEARANCE

CLOTHES

CHARACTER

HOBBIES/
ACTIVITIES

Manner and Mannerism

Instead of only using adjectives to describe a person's character, you can also include examples of the way they speak/look/smile, etc. in order to give a clearer picture and to make the description more lively. *e.g. His blue eyes light up whenever he sees his grandchild.* Although the adjectives **kind** and **affectionate** could be used to describe the person, giving examples of mannerism makes the description more vivid.

15 Read the following descriptions of mannerisms and match them with the adjectives below.

shy, loving, vain, inattentive, aggressive

1 Whenever Roger got involved in an argument, he would shout and become quite violent.
2 Sue is often seen with her children, holding them close, stroking their hair and speaking softly to them.
3 When everybody else is busy studying, Sheila spends her time staring at the ceiling, yawning and playing with her hair.
4 She blushes when she talks to people she does not know and her palms sweat.
5 She always runs her fingers through her golden hair and admires her reflection in the mirror before she goes on stage.

16 Read the model composition and answer the following questions: a) In which paragraph does the writer describe Archie's personality? b) Which phrases describe manner/ mannerism? c) What tenses are used and why? d) What are the writer's feelings about Archie?

Describe a person you will never forget

I first met Archie about thirty years ago when I was a child. Archie was a sailor and a very good friend of my father's. As we lived near a major port, he would visit us whenever his ship came in.

He was a tall, broad man with short brown hair, sparkling blue eyes and a wide smile. His neatly trimmed beard made him look older than he was. He always wore a white sailor's uniform with a dark blue collar and a round white hat.

Archie had a wonderful personality. My brother and I loved it when he told us tall tales of storms and sea monsters. Archie was always telling jokes and his whole body would shake with laughter whenever he found something funny. He was very generous and never forgot to bring us exotic gifts from his travels. There were times, though, when he could be stubborn and he would frown angrily and stamp his feet. He enjoyed being a sailor and spent his whole working life in the Navy, even though many better opportunities came up.

When he was not travelling, he worked on his sailing boat at home. He managed to build it all by himself and went sailing on it in his free time. When he retired, he bought a fisherman's cottage in New Zealand and moved there.

Although we never see him any more, I will always treasure those childhood memories of him.

17 Read the following descriptions and say which quality each one describes.

1 When little Tommy wants a new toy, he screams until his parents buy it for him.
2 Jim tends to stand by himself at parties and hardly ever meets anyone's eye.
3 When Sarah listens to sad music her eyes fill with tears.
4 Whenever he received bad news, John would remain quite still and expressionless.
5 Little Annie makes a face and sticks out her tongue each time she wants to show she doesn't approve of someone.
6 Whenever someone disagrees with Louise, she gets red in the face and shouts until she gets her own way.
7 Jerry is always ready with a smile and a good joke. I've never seen him cross or sad.

Narrative techniques (use of direct speech, weather description, use of dramatic language to create mystery/suspense, reference to feelings/ moods, etc.) can be used when describing people. This will make your composition more interesting to the reader. See how an ordinary beginning can be made more exciting:
Instead of saying: *I first met Steven, the secretary of the manager of Sunnington Ltd, last Monday.*
You could say:

- *A cold wind was blowing down the street last Monday morning as I pushed open the heavy glass door of Sunnington Ltd. Chilled and nervous, I walked up to Mr Tibbs' secretary. A pair of friendly dark eyes met mine. So this was Steven!* (weather description, your feelings, suspense)
- *"Mr Tibbs is at a meeting. Would you like to wait? He'll be about ten minutes." He had a sharp clear voice, and a narrow intelligent face. I could see why Mr Tibbs, the manager of Sunnington Ltd, spoke so highly of Steven.* (direct speech, mystery)

18 Read the following sentences and rewrite them using narrative techniques.

a I was introduced to John McKay, the painter, at Suzie's party on Saturday.
b We first met Mr Simmons on a Tuesday morning when the head teacher introduced him to us as the supply teacher who was taking Mrs Perkins' place.
c I first heard about Tom Cruise two years ago.

19 Read the following models. Which is purely descriptive? Which includes narrative techniques? Give the paragraph outline.

Describe a famous person

MODEL A

Whitney Houston is a person one cannot fail to admire. Over the past ten years she has become both a popular singer and a famous actress, appearing in successful films such as *The Bodyguard.*

Looking at Whitney, it is not difficult to see why she is so popular. She has gorgeous black hair, kind brown eyes and a beautiful smile which lights up her whole face. The elegant clothes she wears always complement her perfect figure.

Whitney has a reputation for being a very warm and generous person. At the same time, she is obviously very determined and can sometimes be rather strong-willed, but this comes from her desire to do things well.

In her free time Whitney, a sociable person, can often be seen at glamorous Hollywood parties. However, she is a very family-minded person who would never let her social life get in the way of her relationship with her daughter.

All in all, Whitney is an incredible woman. Few people manage to fit as much into their lives as she does. It must be exhausting, but she always manages to look fresh and beautiful for the cameras.

MODEL B

I was shaking with fear and nervousness as I waited to interview the star of *The Bodyguard*, Whitney Houston. I was a rather nervous and inexperienced young journalist back then, and interviewing Whitney in a hotel room in Los Angeles was my first big job.

As she opened the door, the first things I noticed about her appearance were her kind brown eyes and her beautiful smile which seemed to light up her whole face. As always, she was dressed elegantly in a stunning long dress which really complemented her perfect figure.

As we chatted, I discovered that Whitney certainly deserves her reputation for being kind and generous and I soon relaxed in her presence. At the same time I noticed a determined side to her, but when I told her that she sometimes comes across as very strong-willed she smiled and told me that this probably came from her desire to do things well.

When she is not working, Whitney, a sociable character, can often be found at glamorous Hollywood parties. Her family life, though, seems to be more important to her than her social life. Her eyes gleamed proudly when I glanced at the photograph of her daughter. Her reaction revealed another side of her character, that of a caring mother.

I felt sad when it was time for me to leave as I had found Whitney to be an incredible woman. I have never met anybody else who could lead such an active life, yet still manage to look fresh and beautiful for the cameras.

20 Write any two of the topics below in the appropriate style using 120-180 words.

1 Your teacher has asked you to write a description of your favourite classmate. Write your description for your teacher.
2 A popular children's TV programme has asked its viewers to send in a description of a relative of theirs, commenting on how this person has influenced them positively or negatively. The best description will win a prize. Write your entry for the competition.
3 Your teacher has asked you to write a composition describing the person you admire most from history. Write your description for your teacher.

UNIT 2 Describing Places/Buildings

1 **Read the following table, then listen to the cassette and tick the information mentioned. Finally, use the table to talk about Sally's trip.**

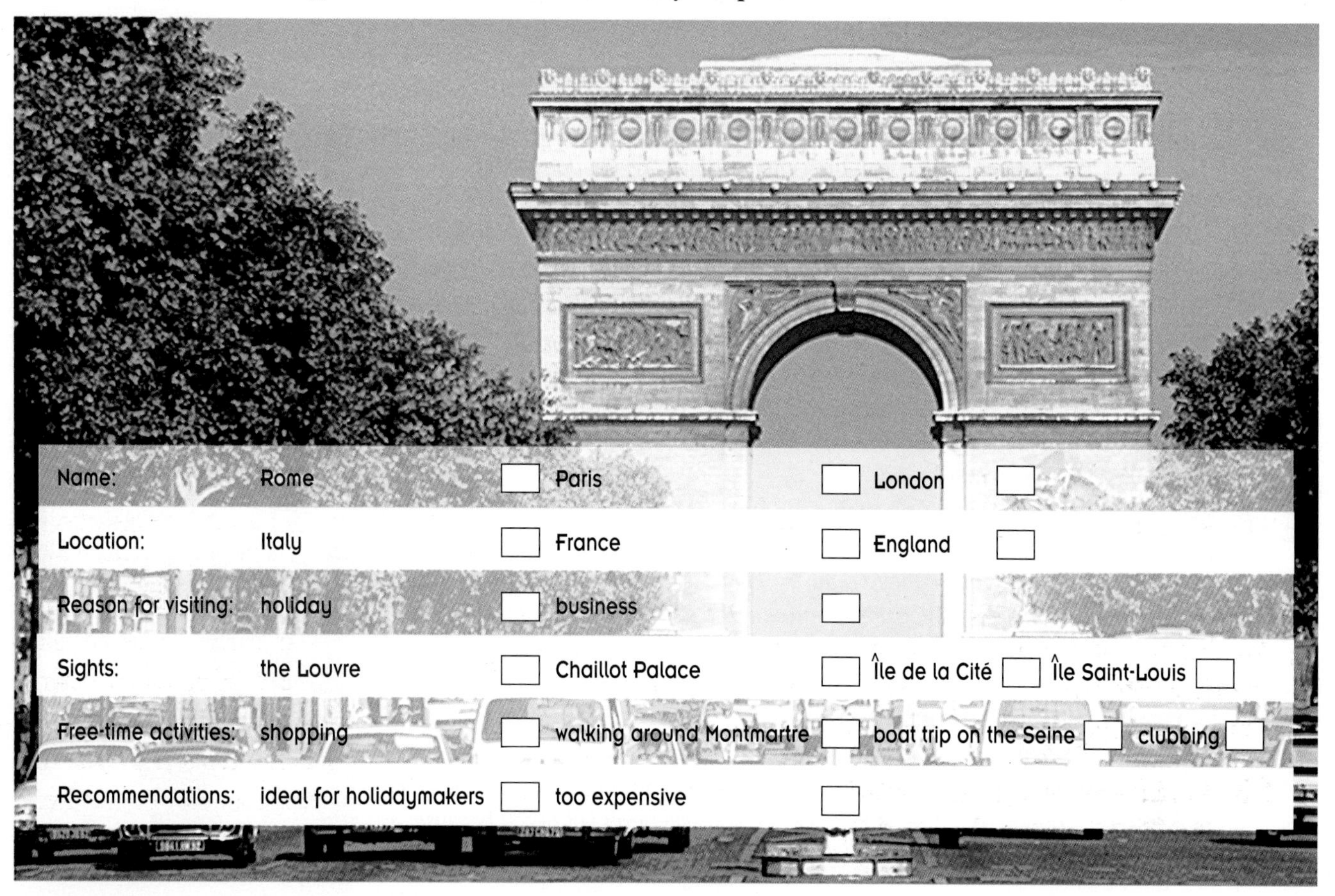

Name:	Rome ☐	Paris ☐	London ☐	
Location:	Italy ☐	France ☐	England ☐	
Reason for visiting:	holiday ☐	business ☐		
Sights:	the Louvre ☐	Chaillot Palace ☐	Île de la Cité ☐	Île Saint-Louis ☐
Free-time activities:	shopping ☐	walking around Montmartre ☐	boat trip on the Seine ☐	clubbing ☐
Recommendations:	ideal for holidaymakers ☐	too expensive ☐		

A descriptive composition about a place or building should consist of:

a) an **introduction** in which you identify it, give its exact location and state the reason for choosing it;

b) a **main body** in which you describe the main aspects of the place or building in detail; and

c) a **conclusion** in which you mention your feelings and your final thoughts about the place or give a recommendation.

Such pieces of writing can be found as articles in newspapers, tourist magazines or brochures, or as part of a story or letter.

Points to consider

- A wide variety of adjectives *(enormous, delightful, etc.)* and adverbs *(horribly, beautifully, etc.)* will make your description more interesting.
- Use of the senses (hearing, sight, smell, taste, touch) as well as narrative techniques to start and finish your composition will make your description more vivid. *e.g. On entering the hospital I was struck by the strong smell of antiseptic.*
- Present tenses should be used when describing a place/building for a tourist brochure. Past tenses should be used when you describe a visit to a place or building which took place in the past. First and second conditionals (will/would) can be used when you describe your ideal house/city, etc.

Introduction

Paragraph 1

set the scene (name & location of the place/building, reason(s) for choosing the place/building)

Main Body

Paragraphs 2, 3

overall look and particular details
(Place: sights, facilities, free-time activities
Building: first look and specific details)

Conclusion

feelings & final thoughts about the place/building and/or a recommendation

2 **Read the model below and write down the topic of each paragraph. Are there any sights of special interest? What can holidaymakers do? Where would you expect to find a description like this?**

name, location (London, England)

Set in the heart of southern England, London is one of the biggest and busiest cities in Europe. A truly international city, London attracts millions of visitors every year from all over the world, yet never loses its own unique charm.

London has many impressive sights to see, ranging from the historical beauty of St Paul's Cathedral and Big Ben to Buckingham Palace and the Houses of Parliament. In this city of contrasts, you can be walking along one of the busiest streets, yet still be less than a mile from one of the many huge, peaceful parks. London is a great cultural centre, too; the National Gallery contains one of the finest collections of classical paintings in the world.

London is also well known for other things apart from its monuments and art galleries. Shoppers will enjoy visiting the department stores on Oxford Street or they could try Harrods, the most exclusive shop in London. For evening entertainment, the choice of theatres is enormous. From the famous Southbank Theatre complex to the smaller theatres of Covent Garden, there is no end of plays to see. Soho and its pavement cafés are also worth visiting.

London is an exceptional place, a truly modern city that has managed to keep its traditional style and sense of history. You may get exhausted in London, but one thing is certain; you will never get bored because, as Dr Johnson once said, "When a man is tired of London, he is tired of life."

3 **Read the model and fill in the missing prepositions. Then, write down the topic of each paragraph. Where would you expect to find a description like this?**

My father works for a large company which is located **1)** .... a huge skyscraper in the city centre.

His office, which is **2)** .... the seventh floor, is spacious and bright due to the natural light coming in **3)** .... the large, full-length windows. It is peaceful too, as a result of its position high **4)** .... the traffic-filled city streets.

The interior is very comfortable. Long curtains hang **5)** .... the ceiling all the way down **6)** .... the pale pink carpet and there are several potted plants **7)** .... one corner of the room. My father's wooden desk with its luxurious black leather chairs, is situated **8)** .... the window so he can look **9)** .... over the city. **10)** .... his chair there is a large wood-panelled cupboard where he keeps his files.

My father's office is a very pleasant working environment and I am sure that working there helps to make his job a lot easier.

4 **The following extracts include descriptions of atmosphere. Read them and underline the phrases which describe use of the senses (i.e. *sight, hearing, etc.*) and identify each sense, *e.g. rustling (hearing)*. Then say which of the extracts could be part of a story and which part of a tourist brochure.**

A Funfair

Even before you enter the funfair you can hear the sound of loud music playing and the shrieks of people on the rides. As you go in, you may be tempted by the smell of fresh popcorn and candy-floss. Lights are flashing and people are bustling everywhere. From the Big Wheel you have a breathtaking view over the whole town.

B Restaurant

The moment we entered the restaurant we began to feel hungry, as the delicious smells of fine cooking reached us from the kitchen. Soft music and quiet conversation created a relaxing atmosphere. A smiling waiter came over to take our order, and we sat back on comfortable cushioned chairs.

C Mountain Village

As you stand on the balcony of the mountain chalet, the cold crisp air makes your skin tingle. All you can hear is the sighing of the wind in the pine trees. The snow-covered mountains in the distance contrast with the thick green forest surrounding the resort.

D Jungle

As we were walking through the jungle, we could hear the rustling of leaves and the screeching of parrots. The scent of wet earth and exotic flowers filled the warm, moist air, which was delightful to breathe.

Two sentences can be joined together by using past participles.

Instead of writing: *The village is surrounded by mountains. The village has a peaceful atmosphere.*

You can write: ***Surrounded** by mountains, the village has a peaceful atmosphere.*

5 **Rewrite the sentences beginning each one with past participles.**

1 Paris is dominated by the Eiffel Tower. Paris is well known for its architecture.

2 The swimming pool is located near the city centre. The swimming pool is very popular with city residents.

3 The hotel is sheltered by trees on either side. The hotel is a favourite with people who want a quiet holiday.

4 The town is hidden beyond a range of mountains. The town is best known for its wine industry.

6 Look at the following list of phrases and match them with the pictures, then identify each sense used. Finally read the example and write short descriptions for any two of the pictures.

crowded streets, glossy green peppers, burning sand, icy cold air, colourful shop signs, snow-covered mountains, whistle of cold wind, crystal-clear water, tall buildings, car horns beeping, fresh scent of pines, swaying palm trees, acrid smell of old tomatoes, hurrying passers-by, colourful stalls, exotic plants, towering peaks, shrill cries of tropical birds, soft snow, cheerfully shouting stallholders, salty sea smell

A

icy cold air (touch) ....

....

....

....

....

....

B

....

....

....

....

....

....

C

....

....

....

....

....

....

D

....

....

....

....

....

....

e.g. *The* ***icy cold air*** *blew around the* ***towering peaks*** *of the* ***snow-covered mountains****. The* ***fresh scent of pines*** *filled the air. I heard the* ***whistle of the cold wind*** *as the* ***soft snow*** *fell around us. No view on earth could be more wonderful.*

7 Look at the following tables, then listen to this person describing what her home town used to be like and what it is like now and complete the missing information. How does the author feel about the changes? Looking at the notes, talk about how the writer's home town has changed. Then write a description of what your town was like forty years ago and what it is like now.

THEN

- fields she used to play in
- small road on the outskirts
- house she grew up in
- old stone bridge
- old houses

NOW

- huge *supermarket*
- major ....
- new ....
- wider................................ bridge
- new ....

e.g. *A huge supermarket has been built in the fields the author used to play in. A motorway has been ...*

- Descriptions of places can be found in travel brochures, letters, magazine articles and stories. They can be written in a formal or informal style depending on whom they are addressed to and how the writer wants to present the description. For example, a description of a place you visited in a letter to a friend would be informal, while a description of a place in a travel brochure could be written in a formal style. It could also be written in a less formal style when the writer wants to sound more persuasive. This can be achieved by writing in a more personal style, addressing the reader directly.

Characteristics of Formal and Informal Style

Formal Style: impersonal style, frequent use of passive voice, complex sentences, use of participles, non-colloquial English, no descriptions of feelings/emotions, short forms acceptable only in quotes, advanced vocabulary
Less Formal Style: personal style, use of idioms, address the reader, chatty descriptions, variety of adjectives, use of short forms, non-colloquial English
Informal Style: personal style, use of colloquial English (idiomatic expressions), use of idioms, use of short forms, chatty descriptions

8 **Read the following extracts and say: a) what style of language has been used for each one, justifying your answers; b) where each extract has been taken from; and c) what the content of each extract is.**

A A visit to the Scottish Highlands is recommended to those who are in search of a peaceful holiday and the opportunity to enjoy some of the most beautiful scenery in the world. One place especially worth visiting for those who are interested in folklore is Loch Ness, famous for its monster.
(formal: impersonal style, complex sentences - part of a travel brochure or magazine article - reasons for visiting)

B The smell of the air, the colours, the bustle of the people and the sound of their excited voices all told Jim he was in Venice. Venice was Jim's favourite city, but this time he wasn't here on holiday. He knew that sooner or later they would find him here. Jim chose a quiet little hotel, tucked away in a back alley. In his room he drew the curtains and sat back, planning his next move.

C Take a trip up the Eiffel Tower to witness the spectacular view, and if you are an art lover you should spend at least a day in the famous Louvre Art Museum. Evenings can be spent in one of the great number of cafés and bistros, where you can sample delicious French cuisine.

D We both feel so relaxed after our holiday in Switzerland, I don't know why we have never been there before. I'd recommend it to anyone who wants to get away from the hustle and bustle of the city and breathe some fresh air. We'll definitely be going back next year.

Narrative techniques can be used when you describe a place or building. You can start or end your description by:

- using your senses to describe the weather, surroundings, etc.
- asking a rhetorical question (a question which expects no answer)
- using direct speech
- describing people's feelings or reactions about the place or building
- using a quotation *(e.g. As Dr Samuel Johnson once said, "When a man is tired of London, he is tired of life.")*
- creating mystery, anticipation or suspense
- addressing the reader

9 **The following sentences are beginnings or endings for a *description of a cottage.* Read them and say which are beginnings and which are endings, then identify the narrative techniques which have been used each time.**

1 Have you ever wanted to live in an old cottage by the Atlantic, with granite walls more than a metre thick, built to withstand the ocean gales? That's where my grandparents live.

2 As I got onto the ferry I repeated to myself, "A mother's love is a blessing no matter where you roam," thinking of the family I was leaving behind in their cosy stone cottage by the sea.

3 I shivered in the chilly drizzle as I turned off the main road past the harbour, heading for my grandparents' cottage. The house, built of granite, seemed to suffer nothing from the strong wind.

4 "Good luck, and may God be with you," said the old man in Gaelic as I glanced back at my grandparents' stone cottage and then walked towards the harbour.

5 I turned off the main road past the harbour and headed for my grandparents' cottage. There it was, its granite walls standing proudly. There was something strange, though. There was no smoke coming from the chimney and it looked abandoned. I shivered as I approached it.

6 As I prepared to leave, I realised that something about visiting my grandparents' cottage always makes me feel safe and secure. Perhaps it's those solid granite walls, or maybe I never feel quite at home or at peace until I'm standing by the old house by the harbour. Whatever it is, that house means more to me than any treasure on earth.

10 **Your teacher has asked you to describe a) a visit to a castle, b) a famous holiday resort in your country. Write possible beginnings and endings for each description, using as many narrative techniques as possible.**

- When you describe places, you may use prepositional phrases and verbs. Prepositional phrases such as ***all around, to the left of, at the top of, as far as the eye can see,*** etc are used to describe static features. Verbs such as ***flow, run, stretch, wind, curve, rise,*** etc are used to describe features which suggest movement.

11 **Underline the words or phrases which describe moving features and circle those which describe static features.**

The grand old house is situated at the end of a long country lane which runs through a small wood. To the left of the house is the coachman's lodge, and as far as the eye can see there is green grass and tall, spreading trees. Beyond the house is a grey rocky mountain and on the other side of it lies a small village with old cottages and a little church in the village square.

12 **Read the following description given in a jumbled order and put the paragraphs in the correct order. Then underline the phrases which involve the senses. Which tenses have been used and why?**

The House of my Dreams

A ☐ My house would have a large, bright kitchen where I could sit quietly at a wooden table admiring the view of the garden through the window. My living room would be simple, with basic furniture like a long soft sofa and two large armchairs. It would also have a fireplace so I could keep warm on cold windy nights. There would also be several wooden bookcases full of books to keep me company. My bedroom would have a four-poster bed with a white linen bed cover and the walls would be painted a soothing pale blue.

B ☐ It would be a small wooden cottage surrounded by a neat green lawn stretching all the way down to a river. There would be colourful flowers gently swaying in the cool breeze and an orchard at the back of the house with trees full of sweet and juicy oranges, apples and pears.

C ☐ If I could choose, I would live in a house just like this with its beautiful natural surroundings and peaceful atmosphere.

D ☐ Imagine waking up to the sound of birds singing in the trees outside and warm sunlight shining through your bedroom window. This is what I dream of when I imagine my ideal house.

13 **Read the model below and correct the mistakes. Write S for spelling, WO for word order, G for grammar, P for punctuation or WW for wrong word. What is the topic of each paragraph?**

G "of" omitted

A visit to a Museum

Standing outside of the British Museum last week, I had ignored the pouring rain as I gazed up at the marble tall columns, unprepared for the dignified beauty of the famous building. Ms Green, our teacher, she hurried us inside, impatient to show to us all the artefacts of the ancient greek and egyptian civilizations which we had studying in our history class.

Inside, the museum was quiet impressive. The gentle hum of voices echoed through huge halls with polished marble floors and sweeping staircases as we were followed Ms Green on tiptoe to the section with the Greek exhibits.

We in admiration gasped at the beautiful sculptures displayed there. The delicate features and graceful bodies of the figures were such lifelike that they looked more as actual people turned to stone than carvings from thousands of years before.

The Egyptian display was even more breathtaking. Huge statues towered above us, gleaming with gold, and beautiful jewellry filled the display cases.

It was like waking from a lovely dream when Ms Green whispered that it was time for us to go. I saw a long, final look, reluctant to live these magical rooms, before I had followed my classmates to the bus waiting and the real world outside.

14 **Write one of the topics below in the appropriate style using 120-180 words.**

1 The town council is running a competition entitled "The house I like most in my neighbourhood". Write a description for the competition.

2 A travel magazine is running a competition and has asked its readers to submit descriptions of a place they think is ideal for holidays. Write your description for the competition.

3 Your teacher has asked you to write about a visit to the zoo. Write your description for your teacher.

UNIT 3 Describing Objects

1 **Read the table below, then listen to the cassette and tick the information mentioned. Which of the two pictures is being described? Finally, use the notes to describe the object.**

Size	small	☐	tall	☐	medium-sized	☐
Weight	light	☐	average	☐	heavy	☐
Age	George III	☐	Louis XIV	☐	Victorian	☐
Shape	rectangular	☐	square	☐	oval	☐
Pattern/Decoration	carvings	☐	emeralds	☐	paintings	☐
Colour	light brown	☐	dark brown	☐	black	☐
Origin	German	☐	French	☐	English	☐
Material	mahogany	☐	granite	☐	stone	☐
Special Characteristics	strap	☐	drawer	☐	label	☐

A

B

- When you describe objects you should be accurate and give a clear picture of what you describe. This means you should give information concerning **size and weight** (*e.g. tall, small, big, heavy, light, etc.*), **shape** (*e.g. rectangular, oval, etc.*) **pattern and decoration** (*e.g. striped, floral, etc.*), **colour** (*e.g. blue, yellowish, etc.*), **origin** (*e.g. Chinese, Italian, etc.*) and **material** (*e.g. cotton, wooden, leather, plastic, woollen, polyester, silk, etc.*) as well as information concerning value, use, quality and special characteristics (*e.g. zip, strap, initials, label, sticker, etc.*).
- Descriptions of objects can be found in leaflets, catalogues, advertisements or as part of letters, stories, reports or articles.
- When you need to use a variety of adjectives to describe an object, they are normally given in the following order: **Opinion, Size/Weight, Age, Shape, Colour, Pattern, Origin, Material**. It is advisable not to use all of them one after the other because your description will not sound natural. Follow this order when you describe objects but give the information in various sentences. *e.g. It's a beautiful small vase. It is white with a flowery pattern and it is made of china.*

2 **List the words under the correct heading as in the example:**

spherical, Polish, platinum, tiny, remarkable, paper, navy blue, enormous, floral, rectangular, wooden, Finnish, breathtaking, brand-new, Oriental, medieval, plain, compact, steel, off-white, antique, heavy, pinkish, woollen, carvings, initials, oval

Opinion	Size/Weight	Age	Shape	Colour	Pattern	Origin	Material	Noun	Special Characteristics
lovely	large	old	square	blue	striped	English	leather	suitcase	with a long strap

3 **Read the following descriptions and underline the adjectives or phrases used to describe each item or the special characteristics they might have. Where could each description have been taken from?**

A My overcoat is dark blue and is made of lambswool. It's fairly old but should be recognised from the initials J.P. sewn on the lining. Should it be found please contact me on ...

B Witnesses reported that the craft appeared to be fifty metres long and resembled a balloon. It was said to be silver in colour with flashing orange lights all around the bottom.

C As he passed by the window, the long steel blade flashed in the moonlight. He kept a firm grip on the heavy, cold handle of the weapon as he slowly made his way to his victim's bedroom.

D This beautiful antique Chinese necklace is guaranteed to enhance even the most classic of outfits. Made of the finest miniature black and white pearls, this masterpiece of craftsmanship is a must for any serious jewellery collector.

4 **Read the following piece of writing and put the adjectives in the correct order. Where do you think this is taken from? What is the topic in each paragraph?**

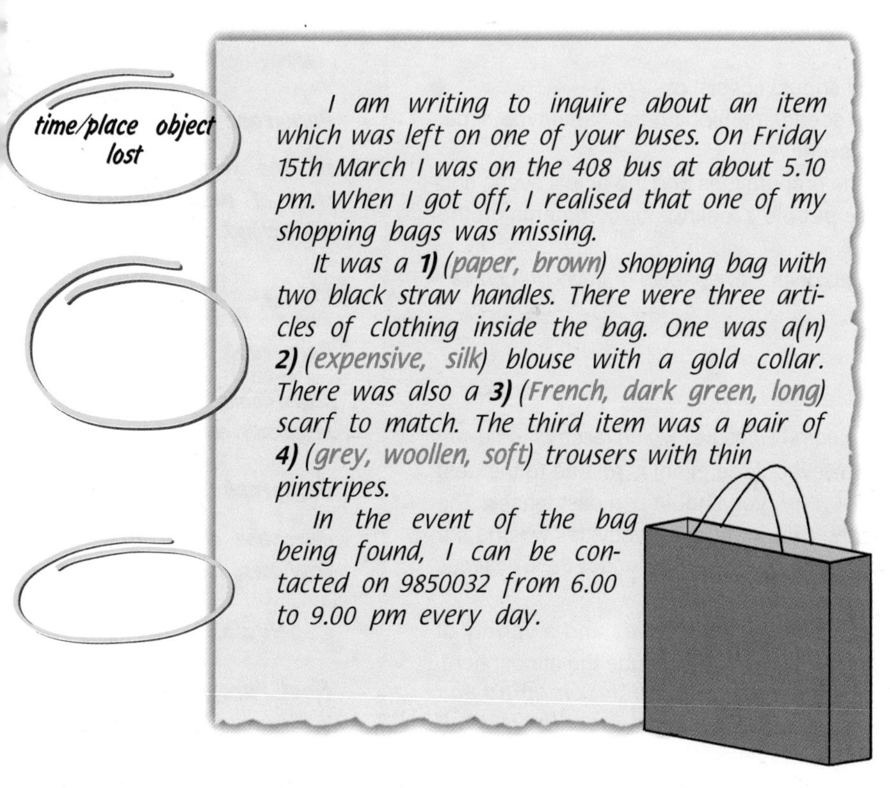

I am writing to inquire about an item which was left on one of your buses. On Friday 15th March I was on the 408 bus at about 5.10 pm. When I got off, I realised that one of my shopping bags was missing.

It was a **1)** *(paper, brown) shopping bag with two black straw handles. There were three articles of clothing inside the bag. One was a(n)* **2)** *(expensive, silk) blouse with a gold collar. There was also a* **3)** *(French, dark green, long) scarf to match. The third item was a pair of* **4)** *(grey, woollen, soft) trousers with thin pinstripes.*

In the event of the bag being found, I can be contacted on 9850032 from 6.00 to 9.00 pm every day.

5 **Match the following adjectives or nouns with the pictures below, then use them to describe each object.**

date display, blue, two straps, leather, rectangular, stamp in the centre, lightweight, Swiss, 18-carat gold band, large blue sapphire, gold and silver bracelet, round-faced, platinum setting, small diamonds, gold

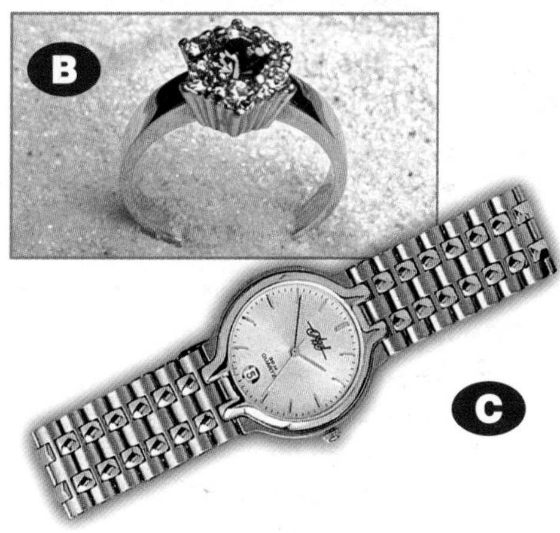

6 **Write one of the following in an appropriate style using 120-180 words.**

1. You have recently bought an item from an antique shop. Write a letter to a friend describing it.
2. You were on flight 302 to Tokyo when you lost an item of luggage. Write a letter to the airline describing the object and giving information on how you can be reached if it is found.

UNIT 4 Describing Festivals/Ceremonies/Celebrations

1 **Read the following table, then listen to the cassette and tick the information mentioned. Finally, looking at the notes, describe the event.**

Reason for celebrating:	fancy dress ☐	birthday ☐	house warming ☐
Time:	last Saturday ☐	yesterday ☐	last Sunday ☐
Guests:	20 ☐	12 ☐	10 ☐
Preparations:	paper plates and cups ☐	flowers ☐	plastic cutlery ☐
	hats ☐	food ☐	jam tarts ☐
	cake ☐	champagne ☐	balloons ☐
Actual day:	sing Happy Birthday ☐	watch videotapes ☐	
	play games ☐	eat and drink ☐	
Feelings:	all enjoyed themselves ☐	some were bored ☐	

- A descriptive composition about an event should consist of:
  a) an **introduction** in which you set the scene, mentioning the name/type, time, place and reason for celebrating this event;
  b) a **main body** in which you describe the preparations and the actual event; and
  c) a **conclusion** in which you describe people's feelings or comments on the event.

  Such pieces of writing can be found in magazines, newspapers or travel brochures, or as part of letters, stories, etc.

Points to consider

- When you describe annual events *(e.g. a carnival/festival which takes place every year)* you should use present tenses. However, if the event is related to the past *(e.g. the carnival/festival you attended last year)*, you should use past tenses. The passive is frequently used to describe the preparations or activities which take place. *e.g. Presents were wrapped in colourful paper and put under the Christmas tree.*
- To make your description more vivid, narrative techniques and a variety of descriptive adjectives can be used to set the scene and describe the atmosphere. *e.g. During the carnival, onlookers line the **crowded** streets, **clapping** and **cheering** as they watch the **brightly coloured** floats and **exotically dressed** dancers go by as the **sound** of traditional Caribbean music fills the air.*

Introduction

Paragraph 1

set the scene (name, time, place of event, reason(s) for celebrating)

Main Body

Paragraph 2

preparations (decorations, rehearsals, etc.)

Paragraph 3

description of the actual event (costumes, food, activities, etc.)

Conclusion

Final Paragraph

feelings, comments, final thoughts

2 **Read the model below and write down the topic of each paragraph. What kind of event is being described? Why has the writer used present tenses? Are there similar events in your country?**

Remembrance Day

Remembrance Day takes place in Britain every year on the Sunday closest to November 11th. It is held to remember all those who died while fighting in World Wars I and II.

Prior to the actual event, many schools and organisations rehearse for the parades which will be held on the day. Paper poppies are sold to the public, and they wear them in their lapels for a week or so before the event. The poppy flower, due to its bright red colour, is used to symbolise the blood shed by the soldiers during the war.

On the actual day, war veterans join the parades, proudly displaying their medals, and they march or are pushed in wheelchairs down the streets to the cheers of the crowds. In the evening there is always a remembrance service, held at the Royal Albert Hall in London, which is televised live. Hymns are sung, speeches are made, and at the end of the service, thousands of poppies are dropped from the ceiling onto the audience below.

Remembrance Day is a very important event. We should respect and feel proud of those people who died fighting in the wars as they played a very significant role in securing our country's freedom.

3 **Form adjectives from the words below and list them in the correct columns. Remember that the spelling of some words may change.**

beauty - joy - glory - colour - nation - marvel - magic - wonder - origin - tradition - excite - entertain - stir - luxury - glitter - sparkle - plenty

- ful	-ous	-al	-ing
beautiful			

4 **Fill in the gaps with one of the words from the list below.**

medals, commemorate, memorial service, parade, traditional costumes, wreath, national anthem, 21-gun salute, veteran, two-minute silence

1. The .... will be held at the Royal Albert Hall.
2. Someone who has fought in and survived a war is called a war ....
3. The audience sang the .... at the beginning of the ceremony.
4. The festival was held to .... fifty years of peace.
5. The Queen laid a .... at the foot of the war memorial.
6. The crowd lined the streets to watch the soldiers marching in the ....
7. It is customary for a .... to be fired at the end of the ceremony.
8. A .... is observed throughout the country as a sign of respect for the people who died in the war.
9. In keeping with the theme of the festival, everyone involved wore ....
10. The veterans proudly displayed their .... as they marched down the street.

5 **Read the model below and put the paragraphs in the right order, then write down the topic of each paragraph.**

"Prom Night"

A ☐ I had been preparing for the prom for months, especially because I was a member of the Prom Committee. We booked an elegant hotel ballroom, had tickets printed, and arranged for a catering company to supply food and refreshments. Four committee members were in charge of the decorations, which reflected the theme of our prom, "Caribbean Moonlight". Two months before the actual night, I found the perfect dress to wear — it made me look like a princess!

B ☐ When I finally returned home, I was tired but extremely happy. It had been a wonderful night, one that would give me pleasant memories for the rest of my life.

C ☐ My high school prom took place on a warm evening in May in a hotel ballroom. The event, which celebrates both the end of high school and the beginning of adulthood, is something every American teenager looks forward to.

D ☐ My parents took pictures of me before I left for the prom. I had a delicate corsage of beautiful orchids on my wrist, without which, my outfit would have been incomplete. The limousine waiting outside took me to the Grand Hotel. All my school friends were there. Together we danced, ate and laughed until one o'clock. I had never stayed out so late before, or had so much fun. My best friend was crowned Prom Queen. We were all very happy for her, if a little jealous, as we watched her dance with the Prom King.

6 **Rewrite the following short paragraphs in the passive. What tenses are used? Why?**

May Day

We cut flowers to make garlands. Others put up the maypole and tie streamers to the top. People decorate floats for the parade. Local bakeries prepare food for the spectators.

....
....
....
....
....
....
....
....
....
....

New Year's Eve

People send out party invitations and buy new outfits. They hang decorations and banners and prepare food. As the clock strikes twelve they open bottles of champagne and make a toast.

....
....
....
....
....
....
....
....

7 **Use of sophisticated adjectives when describing events makes your description more vivid. Read the short texts and fill in the gaps with the adjectives given.**

a) Birthday Party

joyful - sparkling - spacious

The **1)** .... , brightly decorated room had a festive atmosphere. The light from the candles on the cake was reflected in the **2)** .... eyes of the children. Their **3)** .... faces showed their happiness as their parents looked on proudly.

b) Music Festival

spellbound - magical - blinding

1) .... lights lit up the stage as the band walked on. The lead singer sang a **2)** .... love song and the audience sat **3)** .... until the end, then burst into applause.

c) Beer Festival

dazzling - enthusiastic - traditional

The beer festival was officially opened as the band played **1)** .... songs. The **2)** .... crowd cheered with excitement and the sky was illuminated with **3)** .... fireworks.

8 **Read the model about *the Rio Carnival* and replace the adjectives in bold with others from the list. Can you think of other adjectives to be used in their place? Give the paragraph plan. What tenses have been used? Why? Now, write a description of this festival as if you had participated in it. How is your description different from the model below?**

brightly coloured, most spectacular, thrilling, huge, grand, numerous, lively, most impressive

Every year, for the last few days before the forty-day fasting period of Lent, which usually starts at the end of February, visitors from all over the world gather in Rio de Janeiro to witness the **1) nicest** festival in the world – the Rio Carnival.

Preparations for the **2) big** occasion begin months in advance. **3) Nice** costumes are designed and sewn, bands practise their **4) nice** music and ambitious dancers spend hours perfecting their samba routines.

The main part of the carnival takes place in the Sambadrome, a **5) big** stadium where the exotically dressed dancers of **6) many** samba schools compete for prizes awarded for the **7) best** performance and costumes. Outside the stadium, enthusiastic revellers all over the city dance their way through the world's noisiest street party, which continues until the very end of the carnival.

Everyone has fun at the Rio Carnival. The whole city and its hundreds of thousands of visitors look forward to this **8) nice** event every year.

9 **Read the model and correct the mistakes. Write S for spelling, WO for word order, G for grammar, P for punctuation or WW for wrong word. What is the topic of each paragraph? What tenses have been used?**

A Wedding I'll Never Forget *S forgotten*

Sally's wedding day in the local church last July was one not to be forgoten.

The last weeks had been a whirl of bookings dress fittings invitations to be sent, flowers and food to be organised, finding a correct place for the reception – the list seemed endless. But somehow had everything been done on time.

All we gasped when the gleaming, flower-decorated cars turnt into the square and puled up smooth outside the door of the church. The father of Sally, smiling proudly, helped Sally out of the car. She emerged, graceful as a swan, in her romantic white dress. The two little bridesmaids in pink grabbed at the floating veil as the breeze tried to pull it away from them. John smiled hotly as Sally come to stand beside to him. How happy they looked! The service was simple, beautiful and moving. Sallys mother couldn't keep back her tears when the couple exchanged their vows.

After the photographs had taken we all drove off to the reception, which it was held at a local hotel. a delicious dinner was served, toasts were proposed and we all danced far into the night, even after the newlyweds drove away to start their honeymoon.

What an exciting day it had been!

10 **Write one of the topics below in the appropriate style using 120 - 180 words.**

1. An international teenagers' magazine is asking its readers to send descriptions of an important festival in their country. Choose a festival and write your description.
2. Write a description of a national celebration which you have attended.
3. A magazine has asked its readers to submit descriptions of a typical wedding in their country. Write your description for the competition.
4. Your teacher has asked you to describe a birthday party you recently attended. Write your description for your teacher.

UNIT 5 Writing Instructions/Giving Directions/Describing Processes

1 **You are a foreign student in England and want to make a long distance phone call. You don't know how to use the cardphone. Read the instructions, then listen to the cassette and fill in the missing verbs. Finally, cover the instructions and explain how to use the phone.**

- First, **1)** .... the receiver.
- Then **2)** .... your card into the slot.
- **3)** .... for the dialling tone.
- **4)** .... the number carefully.
- After you have finished your call, **5)** .... the receiver down.
- Finally, **6)** .... your card from the machine.

- When writing instructions, describing processes or giving directions, you should give detailed information in chronological order. Write short, clear sentences using the imperative. Such pieces of writing can be found in manuals, leaflets, cookery books or as part of a letter, according to their purpose.

Points to consider

- Each stage of the instructions or process is normally written on a new line. You may either number the various stages or use sub headings to separate them.
- Sequence words such as **first, then, next, as soon as, after that, until**, etc. or expressions/verbs such as **make sure, wait, remember, be careful, do not**, etc. can be used to link pieces of information.
- The passive is used when describing processes. *e.g. The peas* ***are picked*** *and* ***taken*** *to the factory. There they* ***are extracted*** *from the pods.*

Instructions

instructions in chronological order (sub headings can be used)

Recipes

- *ingredients*
- *preparation in chronological order*

2 **Read this extract from a letter, then look at the diagram and fill in the missing words. Now mark the route on the diagram. If you were to travel to Jennifer's town by bus, which route would Jennifer recommend that you follow? Write her directions using words from the list below.**

go/turn left/right, take the first/second etc. turning on the left/right, go past, keep going, opposite

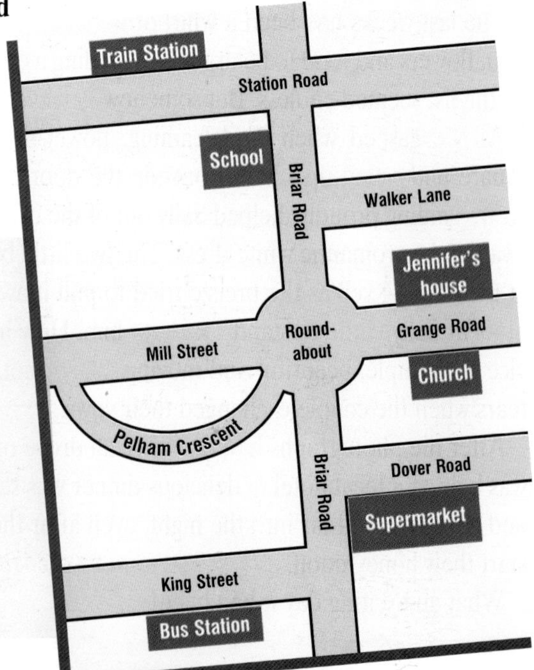

... As you don't drive, I presume that you'll come on the train, so I'll give you directions from the station. 1) .... as you come out of the station and then take the first 2) .... on your right which will take you into Briar Road. Go 3) .... the school on your right and keep going until you get to a roundabout. Take the first turning on the 4) .... at the roundabout and you should find yourself on Grange Road, where I live. My house is on the left-hand side, 5) .... the church.

3 **Read the following steps and put them in the correct chronological order. Then underline the examples of the imperative.**

How to operate a pressure cooker

Preparation

A ☐ Then, fill the pressure cooker with the exact amount of water needed to cook the food.
B ☐ First, make sure the rubber seal is intact inside the lid and the valve on the lid is clean.
C ☐ Check cooking time required.
D ☐ Put the food you want to cook into the pot.

Operating instructions

A ☐ When time is up, switch off ring and remove pressure cooker from ring.
B ☐ Place the lid on the pot and close securely.
C ☐ When the valve begins to spin indicating that the contents are under pressure, lower the heat and begin timing.
D ☐ Remove the lid and serve the food.
E ☐ Put pressure cooker onto the ring.
F ☐ Wait for a few minutes until the pressure valve stops spinning, then carefully release any excess steam by gently lifting the valve.
G ☐ Switch the ring on to desired heat setting.

4 **Fill in the gaps with the verbs from the lists below.**

A *chop, boil, beat, peel, sprinkle, simmer, grate*

1 Before you put the pizza in the oven, ... some cheese and .... it over the top.
2 First you have to .... the potatoes, then put them into a saucepan, cover with water and .... them for about twenty minutes.
3 Turn down the heat and gently .... the sauce for 15 minutes until it thickens.
4 Next, take the carrots and leeks, ... them into small pieces and add them to the mixture in the pan.
5 Put the egg whites into a bowl and .... them until they become stiff.

B *blend, fry, melt, sizzle, grill, slice, bake, stir*

1 Pour the cake mixture into a round tin and .... in a hot oven for about one and a half hours.
2 .... the sausages in a little oil until they start to ...., then remove from the frying pan.
3 Arrange the lamb chops on a tray, season with salt and pepper and .... for 20 minutes, turning them over once.
4 .... a knob of butter in the saucepan, then .... with a tablespoon of flour to make a paste.
5 .... the aubergines thinly, then put a layer on top of the meat.
6 .... the sauce occasionally to prevent it from sticking to the bottom of the pan.

5 **Read the following model and underline the sequence words. What tenses have been used? How is each piece of information given?**

Spaghetti Bolognese

Ingredients

½ kg minced beef
1 large onion, chopped
2 cloves of garlic, crushed
1 tablespoon vegetable oil
1 tin plum tomatoes
1 teaspoonful salt
1 packet spaghetti
200 g Parmesan cheese, grated

Preparation

- First, heat the oil in a large pan and fry the onion and garlic until soft and golden.
- Add the minced beef and stir.
- Cook until the meat is browned.
- Next, mix in the chopped plum tomatoes and salt, then add a glass of water.
- Cover the pan and simmer on a low heat for 50 minutes.
- Meanwhile, boil the spaghetti in a separate saucepan.
- Drain the spaghetti and place it in a serving dish.
- After that, pour the hot bolognese sauce in the centre of the pasta.
- Sprinkle with the Parmesan cheese and serve immediately.

6 **Fill in the gaps with the appropriate verbs from the list below. What is described each time?**

A collect - insert - remove - enter - press - push

- First, **1)** .... the cashcard, with the black stripe facing downwards, into the slot. **2)** .... your PIN number by pressing the buttons.
- Next, select the amount of money you would like to take out, **3)** .... the button marked "enter" and wait. The machine will ask you if you wish to undertake any further transactions. If you do not, **4)** .... "no".
- Your cashcard will then be returned. **5)** .... it from the machine, then **6)** .... your money from the cash dispenser.

B point - hold - look through - put

- First, **1)** .... the video cassette into the slot.
- Next, remove the lens cap by turning it to the left. Make sure the batteries are charged by checking that the battery light is on.
- Then **2)** .... the viewfinder and **3)** .... the camera at the subject you wish to record. **4)** .... the camera steady and press the "record" button.
- When you have finished recording, press the button marked "stop".

Revision Box

7 **Mark the statements True or False justifying your answers.**

1 Examples can be given when describing personality. ☐
2 Present tenses are used to describe someone connected to the present. ☐
3 To describe negative qualities, use mild expressions. ☐
4 You should not use the senses when describing a place. ☐
5 Descriptions of buildings do not include details of the interior. ☐
6 A description of a place in a travel brochure is always written in formal style. ☐
7 Past tenses are used to describe an event you personally attended. ☐
8 Chronological order is not important when giving instructions. ☐

8 **Write one of the topics below in the appropriate style using 120-180 words.**

1 A cookery magazine is running a competition, asking its readers to submit a recipe for a typical dish from their country. Write your recipe.
2 You are working for a company which sells electrical appliances. You have been asked to write simple instructions for operating a) a CD player, and b) a camera, to be included in the manuals.
3 A friend of yours is visiting your town and wants to visit you. Write a letter to him/ her, giving directions to reach your house.

UNIT 6 Narratives - Stories

1 **The pictures below are from a story entitled *"Rescued!"* Try to put them in the correct order, then listen to the cassette and check your answers. Finally, retell the story in your own words.**

- A narrative can be written in the first or the third person and describes a series of events, either imaginary or based on your own experience. A good narrative should consist of:
  a) an **introduction** in which you set the scene (people involved, time, place) in an interesting way to catch the reader's attention and make him/her want to continue reading your story;
  b) a **main body** consisting of two or more paragraphs in which you develop your story; and
  c) a **conclusion** in which you can refer to people's feelings, comments and reactions or consequences. The more unpredictable your conclusion is, the longer-lasting the impression it will make on the reader.

  This type of writing can be found in novels, articles, witness statements, etc.

Points to consider

- You should never start writing your story before you have decided on a plot.
- Sequence of events is very important. Use time words such as: **at first, before, until, while, during, then, after, finally,** etc.
- Use of various adjectives (disgusted, exhilarating, etc.) and adverbs (fearlessly, surprisingly, etc.) to describe feelings and actions, as well as use of direct speech and a variety of verbs, will make your story more exciting to read.
- Be careful with the tenses you choose. You can use **Past Continuous** to set the scene *(e.g. It **was raining** hard and the wind **was blowing** as Jonathan drove towards the small cottage.)*, **Past Simple** to describe the main events of the story. *(e.g. Jonathan **opened** the garden gate and **went** through the garden towards the front door. He **knocked** on the door but there **was** no answer.)* or **Past Perfect** to give the background of the story *(e.g. Jonathan **had been planning** to visit the old cottage for months before he was able to do so)*. **Present** and **past participles** can also be used. *e.g. **Startled,** he went round the house towards the back door.*
- Descriptions of people, places, objects or events and descriptive techniques can be used in a narrative when you want to emphasise specific parts of your narration.

Introduction

Paragraph 1
Set the scene (who — where — when — what)

Main Body

Paragraphs 2 - 4

Development

(describe incidents leading up to the main event and the event itself in detail)

Conclusion

Final Paragraph

End the story

(refer to moods, consequences, people's reactions, feelings, comments)

2 **Read the model below, which begins with the words *"Sleep tight, Scottie,"*... and write down the topic of each paragraph. In which person is the story written? Underline the parts of the story where descriptive techniques are employed. Underline the time words, adjectives, adverbs and direct speech. Has the writer used a variety of adjectives and adverbs, or are the same words used several times?**

set the scene (Scottie in bed - ball of light enters his room)

"Sleep tight, Scottie," his mother said as she kissed him goodnight and turned off the light. As soon as she had closed the door behind her, Scott was fast asleep. He was completely exhausted after spending the whole afternoon assembling his new train set and then watching it go around the tracks and through the tunnels. Suddenly, a ball of brilliant yellow light shot past the window. Scott woke with a start when the ball entered his room. The light was so bright that he had to shut his eyes.

When he opened them, he saw a strange, little man, about a foot tall, with orange skin and huge blue eyes. Scott, not the least bit frightened, said in a friendly voice, "Hello, I'm Scott. Who are you?" The miniature man said nothing, but picked up a battery from the untidy heap of toys on the floor. He started running around the room, pointing urgently at the rest of Scott's toys. "What do you want?" asked Scott, who was puzzled.

The man began shaking the battery frantically, and Scott realised that that was what he wanted. Scott opened all his toys, took out the batteries and piled them on the floor. Immediately gathering up all the batteries, the little man leapt onto the window sill, smiled warmly at Scott and disappeared.

When Scott woke up the next morning, he thought about his unusual dream. He stared at his train set before jumping out of bed and trying to switch it on. Nothing happened. Then Scott realised that it had no batteries ... and there were no batteries in any of his other toys, either.

Techniques to begin or end a story

A good beginning is as important as a good ending. A good beginning should make your reader want to go on with your story. A good ending will make your reader feel satisfied.

You can start your story by:

a. describing weather, surroundings, people, etc. using the senses
b. using direct speech
c. asking a rhetorical question (a question which expects no answer)
d. creating mystery or suspense
e. referring to your feelings or moods
f. addressing the reader directly

You can end your story by:

a. using direct speech
b. referring to your feelings or moods
c. describing people's reactions to the events developed in the main body
d. creating mystery or suspense
e. asking a rhetorical question

Note that more than one technique can be used in the beginning or ending of your story.

3 **Which of the following beginnings and endings are more interesting? Why?**

BEGINNINGS...

A I woke up and got out of bed. I had a shower, ate breakfast and left.

B Bright morning sunlight shone through my bedroom window when I woke. I lay there lazily for a few minutes, then jumped out of bed and stepped under the hot water of the shower. The smell of coffee drifted through from the kitchen.

...ENDINGS

A Exhausted and soaked to the skin, I slammed the front door behind me. I threw myself onto my bed, stared into the darkness and thought bitterly, "Why me?"

B At last I was home again, and soon went to bed. It had been a tiring day.

4 **Read the main body of the story below, as well as the different beginnings and endings. Refer back to the theory box on page 28 and decide which techniques have been used in each of the beginnings and endings.**

BEGINNINGS...

b 1 "Oh gosh, look at the time!" gasped my flatmate Caroline as she nudged me awake. We gathered up our books and sleepily made our way to the library car park.

☐☐☐ 2 It was a damp, chilly night when Caroline and I eventually left the library. As soon as I stepped outside I shivered, feeling that something strange was about to happen.

☐☐☐ 3 You know those spring nights that are still really cold and damp? Well, I'll tell you what happened to my friend Caroline and me, on a night just like that.

We had been studying in the library for hours and we just wanted to get home and go to sleep. Normally, I would take the long way home, to avoid driving past the old Bradford estate. However, that night I was so exhausted that I forgot all about it. Before I knew it, we found ourselves driving down the long, winding road which goes past the estate. Since it was pitch dark and my headlights could barely cut through the thick fog, I was driving fairly slowly. The silence was broken as we heard a tapping sound coming from the darkness ahead.

Suddenly, an elderly man dressed in a black suit appeared at the side of the road, limping along with a wooden cane. He turned and faced us, and began to approach the car. His wrinkled face, piercing dark eyes and toothless grin gave him a horrifying appearance. We quickly locked all the doors and kept driving. The old man tried to block our path by stepping out in front of the car, but I swerved and sped off.

...ENDINGS

b☐☐ 1 Safe at home, we decided we had probably imagined the whole thing. The next morning, however, as we opened the front door to leave for the college, we both froze with shock. There, propped up against the wall, was a long wooden cane.

☐☐ 2 The next day in class, our professor showed us some slides of the town's early founders. He clicked his slide machine to the next picture — and guess whose face flashed onto the screen?

☐☐☐ 3 The next day I told my professor what had happened, and to my surprise his eyes filled with tears. "The man you've described was my father," he mumbled. "He died at that place twenty years ago."

5 **Match the beginnings with the endings. Which techniques have been applied? Which pair is not very successful? Rewrite this pair, applying the techniques mentioned before.**

BEGINNINGS...

1 It was very late. John couldn't see because it was dark. He was afraid.

2 The snow lay like frosty icing on a Christmas cake, its crisp, new whiteness covering the garden like a soft fluffy blanket. It was still snowing, frozen crystals falling gently from the heavy grey sky.

3 Why is it that the most important changes in our lives happen when we least expect them to? My life had settled into a comfortable, satisfying routine when suddenly everything changed.

...ENDINGS

A Looking back at what happened I always feel a sense of wonder and awe. But then again, life's like that, isn't it?

B John ran out of the house. There was a policeman outside. John felt safe.

C We all felt a deep sense of loss when the last traces of the snow had melted away, realising what a special gift we'd been given and how much fun and laughter it had brought us. It had been such a fleeting visit, but one we weren't likely to forget for a very long time.

Before you start writing your story it is absolutely necessary to plan it. This means that you should decide on a plot line and then start developing it. You can link the events with time words such as: **first, until, when, before, after, eventually, at once, finally,** etc.

6 **Read the following short texts and fill the gaps with linking words or phrases from the lists below.**

A *as soon as, at last, immediately, meanwhile, then, when, while*

The aeroplane had only been in the air for about twenty minutes **1)** .... suddenly it began to dive towards the ground. **2)** .... the passengers began to panic. **3)** .... the flight attendants realised what was happening, they did their best to calm everyone down, **4)** .... the plane continued to lose altitude.

5) ...., in the cockpit, the pilot was struggling to control the plane. **6)** .... it righted itself and he sighed with relief. The flight **7)** .... continued without any further problems.

B *after, before, finally, since, then, when*

There had never been a storm like it **1)** .... – at least not **2)** .... the great flood in 1962. Kevin was trying to steer his car through the pouring rain **3)** .... all of a sudden his car stopped. The engine continued to run for a few seconds, **4)** .... coughed twice and fell silent.

Reluctantly, Kevin got out of his car and watched it sink slowly into the mud at the side of the road. **5)** .... staring at his useless car for a few minutes, he **6)** .... stuck his hands into his pockets, bent his head and began the long walk home.

Now number the events below in the order in which they happened.

Plot line A	Plot line B
☐ The passengers panicked.	☐ The car stopped.
☐ The pilot managed to control the plane.	☐ Kevin walked away.
☐ The aeroplane started falling.	☐ The car sank in the mud.
☐ The flight continued.	☐ Kevin got out of the car.
☐ The flight attendants calmed the passengers..	☐ Kevin was driving in the rain.

7 **Decide on various plot lines for the following sentences which end stories.**

a. It was the worst flight I had ever experienced.
b. I would never go back there again.
c. "You're fired!" he shouted.

8 **Read the beginning and ending of the following story, then look at the pictures and decide on the events you will describe in the main body, listing them in chronological order. Then, using this list, write the missing main body.**

James couldn't believe his eyes. He checked the figures again, hoping he had made a mistake. £20,000 in debt! What could he do? ....
....
....
....
....

Early one morning, three months later, out of work and bankrupt, Joe left his flat carrying a black case. He made his way to the local underground station, found a sheltered spot and laid a hat on the ground. He then took his shiny saxophone out of its case and began to play.

Avoid using simplistic adjectives or adverbs *(e.g. good, bad, nice, well,* etc.) as these will make your composition sound uninteresting. Try to use more sophisticated adjectives or adverbs *(e.g. luxurious, extravagant, threateningly,* etc.) which will make your composition more exciting to read. A variety of verbs *(e.g. murmur, whisper, mutter* instead of *"say")* will make your story more lively.

*e.g. "Hide it," he **murmured** and put a small box into my hand. (instead of 'said')*
*She was **wandering** the streets aimlessly, trying to make a decision. (instead of 'walking')*

9 **The following adjectives or adverbs can be used instead of other simplistic ones. Put them into the correct box. Can you think of any more words?**

absolutely, delightful, enormous, entirely, horrible, massive, miniature, microscopic, superb, terrific, thoroughly, horrifying, extremely, gigantic, tiny, nasty, disgusting, huge, terrible, wonderful, unpleasant, fabulous

BIG	
SMALL	
VERY	
BAD	
GOOD/NICE	

Now replace the words in bold in the following paragraphs with suitable words from the boxes above.

A

The **1) big** old castle stood at the top of a(n) **2) big** mountain in the middle of a(n) **3) big** forest. I was **4) very** terrified as I approached and jumped with fright when I heard a(n) **5) bad** scream from the direction of the castle. My heart was in my mouth as I knocked on the **6) big** front door, and the sound of **7) small** scurrying feet behind the door made me imagine **8) big, 9) very bad** rats running away to hide. I wanted to run away, too, but I was **10) very** exhausted, and had to find somewhere to sleep for the night.

B

It was a(n) **1) nice** evening, and after a(n) **2) nice** sunset the stars were a million **3) small** points of light in the sky. "A(n) **4) nice** end to a(n) **5) very 6) nice** day," Brian thought to himself; and after the **7) bad** week which had just passed, he was **8) very** pleased to breathe a(n) **9) big** sigh of relief and put the **10) bad** memories behind him.

10 **The adverbs below describe the way a person might speak or act. Explain what each adverb means, then choose suitable words from the list to complete the sentences.**

sarcastically, angrily, threateningly, frantically, hurriedly, miserably, confidently, suddenly, urgently, nervously, patiently, calmly

1 The woman on the third-floor balcony of the burning building waved her arms .... to attract the fireman's attention.
2 "Get out of here!" Bill shouted ...., his face turning red.
3 "My dog has run away!" the little girl sobbed ....
4 ...., without any warning, her guide spun round and held a knife to her throat.
5 The detective looked at him in disbelief. "Oh, yes, of course a criminal like you wouldn't want £5 million," he said ....
6 She gathered her papers together .... and rushed off to the meeting, which had already begun.
7 "If you tell anyone, you'll be sorry," said the kidnapper ....
8 "Don't worry, I'll kill the dragon," the knight said .... to the king.

11 Put the following verbs into the correct boxes. Try to think of further words to add to each box. Now use suitable words from the boxes to complete the following sentences.

gaze - dash - giggle - hiss - murmur - peer - stroll - wander - yell - sigh - chuckle - mutter - peep - moan - shriek - grin - whisper - exclaim - rush

Walk/Run	....	Say	....
...*dash*...........	....	....	....
....	....	....	....
....	....	....	....

Look	....	Smile/Laugh	....
....	....	....	....
....	....	....	....

WALK/RUN

1 We .... lazily along the waterfront, enjoying the warm sunshine as we watched the fishermen mending their nets.

2 At the sound of the doorbell she .... eagerly to the front door, excited to be meeting him again after so many years.

SAY

3 "Stupid old fool!" he .... angrily to himself, pushing rudely past the elderly man limping down the steps.

4 "Oh, well," Jill .... "perhaps it doesn't really matter – but I wish you'd asked me first before telling everyone about it."

5 "Don't look round now, but I'm sure that man sitting behind us is the escaped prisoner I was reading about in the paper," I .... nervously to John.

6 "Help!" Karen .... hysterically. "Somebody help me!"

LOOK

7 The couple .... lovingly into each other's eyes, completely unaware of the people hurrying past.

8 Kevin .... through the windscreen, hardly able to see where he was going in the pouring rain.

SMILE/LAUGH

9 David .... cheerfully as he waved to the crowd, accepting their applause for the magnificent race he had run.

10 Sally and Lynne .... with embarrassment when the two boys crossed the room and asked them to dance.

12 Rewrite the short paragraphs replacing the words in bold using words from Ex. 11 as in the example.

1 "Here he comes!" **said** Carla, **looking** anxiously through the sunlit blinds. "And he's got a parcel!" The postman was **smiling** as he **walked** up the path.

e.g. "Here he comes!" ***shrieked*** *Carla,* ***peering*** *anxiously through the sunlit blinds.*

2 "The plane is going to crash," **said** Steve. Everyone in the air traffic control room **looked** at him. Steve **ran** back to his monitor and put on his headset. "Why on earth don't they answer?" he **said**. "I'm afraid there's nothing we can do to help them now," he **said**.

Use of the senses (sight, smell, touch, hearing, taste) to set the scene or describe people, places, events or objects involved in your story helps to increase the reader's interest.

13 **Underline the words or phrases which are used to describe senses. What sense does each refer to?**

1 Maitland staggered across the road, hardly aware of the hooting cars and foul-smelling exhaust fumes. The cut on his arm was burning, his head was throbbing with pain, and the salty taste of blood filled his mouth. A police car screeched around the corner, siren wailing and lights flashing, and Maitland dashed into a dark doorway.

2 It was a hot, lazy afternoon and, from where I sat on the shady verandah, I could see the purple mountains in the distance. The fragrant flowers around me blazed with colour as, sipping my sharply sweet lemonade, I listened to the gentle hum of crickets and twittering of birds. A soft, cool breeze brushed my skin while I enjoyed the smell of the rich earth. Suddenly, a familiar, annoying buzz sounded in my ear.

14 **Look at the following list of verbs, all of which refer to sounds and light, and fill in the correct verbs in the gaps below. Some verbs may be used more than once. Which of these could be used in a story entitled *"A Haunted House"*?**

bang, crackle, creak, flash, flicker, hoot, howl, pound, rattle, rumble, roar, rustle, twinkle, wail

1 leaves/paper ....
2 wind/wolves ....
3 chains ....
4 stars ....
5 lions/crowd/fire ....
6 thunder/lorries ....
7 waves/rock music/heart ....
8 sirens/cats ....
9 staircase/floorboards ....
10 flames ....
11 doors/guns/explosion ....
12 owls/cars ....
13 candles ....
14 lightning ....

15 **Look at the pictures, and decide on the plot line of the story. Then, using words from Ex. 9 - 14 write a story entitled *"The Haunted House."***

16 **Read the story below. The paragraphs are in the wrong order, and the story has no punctuation. Number the paragraphs in their correct order, and punctuate them, then underline the phrases which are used to describe the senses as well as the time words.**

The most exciting experience of my life

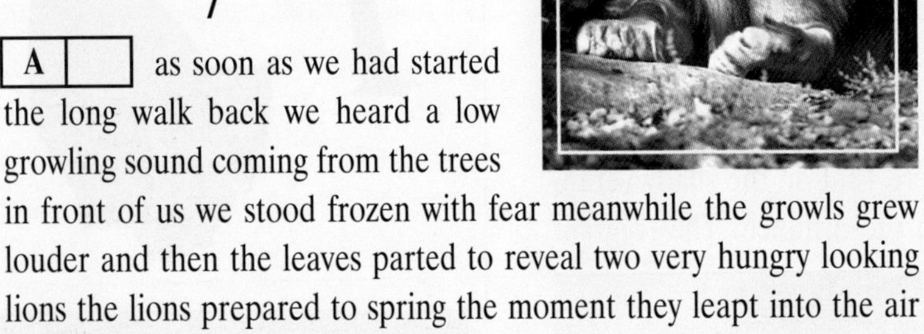

A ☐ as soon as we had started the long walk back we heard a low growling sound coming from the trees in front of us we stood frozen with fear meanwhile the growls grew louder and then the leaves parted to reveal two very hungry looking lions the lions prepared to spring the moment they leapt into the air we threw ourselves to the ground the lions sailed over our heads and plunged into the narrow valley

B ☐ have you ever wished that your holidays were more exciting i certainly had until my experience on the first day of a photo safari holiday i took with my friend howard last june

C ☐ as we shakily made our way back to the camp we couldn't believe what a lucky escape we had had howard wiped the sweat from his forehead and said maybe its time to go back to good old fashioned beach holidays

D ☐ we had been walking through the undergrowth for some time when our guide suddenly stopped in his tracks directly in front of us was a narrow valley almost hidden by creepers and leaves phew that was close said howard i suppose we'll have to turn back now

E ☐ the morning sun was blazing as we set out on our first trip into the jungle a guide led howard and me into what we hoped would be a day of successful photography

17 **Read the sentences, then listen to the story on the cassette and put the events into the correct order. Finally, retell the story in your own words.**

Crime doesn't pay

A ☐ They got out of the car and walked towards the cabin.

B ☐ Sarah heard someone open the front door of her house.

C ☐ The man carried Sarah into the empty cabin.

D ☐ Sarah tried to escape through the window.

E ☐ The man was caught.

F ☐ The man drove Sarah to a wooded mountainside.

G ☐ Sarah stole the money and hid it in her wardrobe.

H ☐ Sarah collapsed onto the icy snow.

I ☐ A man entered Sarah's room and forced her out of the house into his car.

When writing a narrative you can use flashback narration. This means you can start your story at a certain point in time (often a very exciting moment), then go back in time and describe events which happened before this time (usually in Past Perfect), lead the reader up to the specified time, then go on with your story and bring it to a conclusion.

18 **Read the story and put the verbs into the correct tenses.**

A flight to remember

The wheels of the jet screeched briefly as they **1)** .... (hit) the runway, waking me from a long pleasant sleep.

"Well, we're here," smiled the woman sitting next to me, "Is this your first visit to Rio de Janeiro?" I **2)** .... (stare) at her in disbelief. "Rio?" I **3)** .... (gasp). "We're supposed to be in Rome!" But when I **4)** .... (look) out of the window and saw the unmistakeable view of Sugar Loaf Mountain and the huge statue of Christ in the distance I **5)** .... (realise) that I **6)** .... (make) a terrible mistake.

Earlier that day, I **7)** .... (arrive) late at Heathrow Airport in London after being delayed in heavy traffic. As soon as I had checked in and grabbed my boarding pass I **8)** .... (rush) frantically to Gate 12 where the flight attendant was just about to close the door to the narrow tunnel. Fortunately she **9)** .... (see) me coming and waved me through quickly as there was no time to check my ticket. Completely exhausted from all the rushing, I fell asleep within seconds of sitting down, relieved that I hadn't missed my flight to Rome.

"How on earth have I ended up in Rio?" I **10)** .... (wonder). I **11)** .... (pull out) my boarding pass and **12)** .... (read) it again, this time carefully. "Heathrow to Rome, Gate 21," it said – 21 not 12!

Eventually, after I **13)** .... (explain) my embarrassing situation to the airport officials, I was finally put on a flight to my original destination – Rome. Needless to say, I **14)** .... (not/sleep) a wink during that flight!

Now look at the list of events as they appeared in the story above and put them into the correct chronological order. Retell the story without using flashback narration.

A		The plane landed.
B		I woke up.
C		A fellow passenger said we were in Rio.
D		I arrived at the airport.
E		I checked in.
F		I rushed to Gate 12.
G		I took my seat on the plane.
H		I fell asleep.
I		I read my boarding pass carefully.
J		I explained my situation to the airport officials.
K		I was put on a flight to Rome.

19 **Read the following story which begins with the words *"Someone from the hospital called; it sounded urgent."* and correct the mistakes. Write S for spelling, WO for word order, WW for wrong word, G for grammar or P for punctuation.**

G *wait*

"Someone from the hospital called; it sounded urgent. It's your wife. Maybe you should ..." Paul didn't waited for the secretary to finish.

He turned pale and broke into a cold sweat, then did his way hurriedly back to the car park, jumped into his car and drived crazily through the slow traffic. He hard noticed the honking of horns, the screeching of breaks or the other drivers yelling furiously at him. "Please, please let her be all right," he kept saying to himself.

Minutes later, the doors of the emergency department opened and he found him in the cold reception lounge. He pushed to the front of the queue and asked for his wife. the receptionist patiently scanned the computer screen and then directed him to Room 12. Without to thanking her, he dashed for the lift. Heart pounding, Paul his eyes closed for a moment, praying. He dreaded what he was about to find.

The door opened onto a dimly lighted corridor. Paul walked towards Room 12 and nervous pushed the door open. She was laying in bed, exhausting. She sleepily opened her eyes and murmured, "hello, darling. Sory I couldn't wait. Its a boy."

20 **Read the notes below for a story entitled *"The Visitors"*, put them into the correct chronological order, then tell the story. Now, change the order of the notes to make use of flashback narration. Which note will you start your story with? Write your story using flashback narration.**

A		Doorbell rang – Ruth ... with 3 children and a dog!
B		Finally, 2 weeks later, Ruth said they were going.
C		First night, I slept on sofa; children played loud music on radio all night.
D		Phone call from friend, Ruth – wanted to stay with me "for a few days".
E		Will never invite old friends to stay again – and don't want to see Ruth again for another fifteen years.
F		Came home from work next day – garden destroyed, window broken, furniture covered in marmalade.
G		Waved goodbye, closed door behind me – relieved to be alone again.
H		Last time I saw Ruth was fifteen years ago; thought how nice it would be to spend a few days together.

Revision Box

21 **Mark the statements True or False justifying your answers.**

1 A story cannot begin with direct speech. ☐
2 Time words should be used in stories. ☐
3 Stories should not combine description and narration. ☐
4 Use of the senses to set the scene should be avoided. ☐
5 Punctuation and paragraph planning are essential in stories. ☐
6 Sequence of events is not important in stories. ☐
7 You can narrate a story by moving back in time. ☐
8 When writing a story, past tenses should be used. ☐

22 **Read the following topics, decide on the plot line, then write any of them in 120 - 180 words.**

1 You have decided to enter a short story competition. You should write a story ending with the words: *"It was only then that I realised they had mistaken me for someone else."*
2 A magazine is running a competition for the best short story starting with the words: *"Who can this man be?" Sheila wondered as she looked at the stranger standing at the front door."*
3 A magazine is running a competition for the best short story entitled *"A Disastrous Evening"*. Write your story.

UNIT 7 Witness Statements

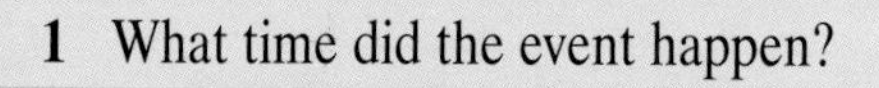

*12

1 Read the following questions, then listen to the cassette and answer them. What event is described? Looking at the notes, retell the incident.

1 What time did the event happen?

2 Where was the witness going?

3 What did the witness see?

4 What was the burglar wearing?

5 Where did the burglar go?

6 Was there anyone in the house?

7 How did the burglar manage to get into the house?

8 What did the witness do then?

9 What happened in the end?

A witness statement describes an incident as it was experienced by someone who was there, whether involved or not, at the time the event happened. It is always in the first person and is normally rather formal in style.

A good witness statement should consist of:

a) an **introduction** in which you mention the time and place the incident happened as well as the people involved.

b) a **main body** in which the incident is described clearly in detail. Accurate descriptions of people or objects involved in the incident should be included.

c) a **conclusion** which includes the final result of the incident.

Such pieces of writing are addressed to the police, insurance companies, courts, etc.

Points to consider

- Information should be given in chronological order. Events should be linked together with appropriate time words.
- Evidence can be supported by hypothesis (your own ideas about what must have happened). To join hypothesis and evidence you can use words such as: *because, so, therefore,* etc. *e.g. We found no fingerprints; therefore, the burglars must have been wearing gloves.*

Introduction

Paragraph 1

Set the scene (time, place, people involved in the incident)

Main Body

Paragraphs 2 - 3

description of the main events and people involved, hypotheses and evidence

Conclusion

Final Paragraph

final results of the incident

2 **Read the following witness statement and write down the topic of each paragraph. What is the witness statement about? In which person is it written? What examples of hypothesis have been used?**

As I was making my nightly rounds on Monday evening, I noticed a faint light coming from a third floor window of Scope Ltd. It must have been about 11.15 pm because I had checked my watch just minutes earlier. As I was proceeding to the main entrance to check for signs of a break-in I witnessed two men running out of the door towards the gate.

Both men appeared to be in their mid thirties and were rather tall with short brown hair. They were wearing dirty ripped jeans and black leather jackets. They must have been professionals because they managed to get in and out of the building without setting off the sophisticated alarm system. I tried to pursue them but was unable to catch them because they got into a black Ford Cortina and drove off in the direction of Tackinton.

About two minutes later I heard a bomb explode and saw flames coming out of the third floor windows. The fire soon spread to other floors, and the whole building was in flames within minutes.

I immediately called the police and the fire brigade who arrived at 11.30.

3 **Decide which sentence is a hypothesis and which is evidence, then join the sentences.**

1 The burglars managed to de-activate the burglar alarm. The alarm didn't go off.
...The burglars must have de-activated the burglar alarm (hypothesis) because the alarm didn't go off (evidence) ...
2 There were no signs of a break-in. The back door was left unlocked.
3 The kidnappers got scared. They let the victim go before the ransom was paid.
4 The security guard didn't try to stop the robbery and disappeared afterwards. He was a member of the gang.
5 The burglars had been watching the house for days. They knew that the owners were away.
6 The thief was a store employee. Money was stolen from the hidden safe.

4 **Link the sentences using appropriate words/phrases from the list below, as in the example.**

at the same time, meanwhile, later, all of a sudden, then, while, as, when, at once, immediately, finally, eventually, as soon as

1 I was waiting in the bank. Two men carrying guns came in. Another man was waiting outside in a car.
... As I was waiting in the bank, two men carrying guns came in. Meanwhile, another man was waiting outside in a car....
2 I turned the corner. I noticed a woman running down the street. A policeman came out of a building and ran after her.
3 The car skidded. It crashed into the one in front. I heard the sound of glass breaking. Both drivers jumped out.
4 I smelt something burning. I was watching TV. I decided to investigate. I discovered that my oven was on fire.
5 I saw a man with a gun. I panicked. I started screaming for help. The man ran away down the street.

5 Read the following notes then try to expand them into a proper witness statement. Start the statement as shown in the example.

- Tuesday evening about 7.00 pm
- B27 road
- flashing lights
- car engine stopped
- got out of car
- huge, grey metal object 100 metres away
- thought it must be a UFO
- it spun around quickly and then disappeared
- looked at watch, but it had stopped
- car started again, drove back home

"I was driving along the B27 road on Tuesday evening ...

....

....

....

6 Read the following witness statement and fill in the missing words from the list below. Then look at the diagram below and using words from the list, describe the incident as if you had been a witness to it.

injured, crashed, speeding, colliding, swerved, passer-by, direction, skidded, damaged

I was waiting for the 7 o'clock bus to go to work on Tuesday morning when I saw a black Sierra come **1)** .... down the road.

Just as it approached the roundabout, the driver seemed to lose control. The car spun round and **2)** .... into a red Ford Fiesta which was coming in the opposite **3)** .... The car behind the Fiesta **4)** .... in order to avoid **5)** .... with the two cars but **6)** .... on the oily surface and crashed into a sign. I ran to help the drivers get out of their cars while a **7)** .... called for an ambulance. When we managed to get the driver out of the black Sierra he smelt of alcohol, so he must have been driving while drunk.

The ambulance arrived and took the three **8)** .... drivers to hospital. All three cars were badly **9)** ....

7 Choose one of the topics below and write it in the appropriate style using 120 - 180 words.

1. While shopping in a supermarket, you notice someone stealing goods. You have been asked to report the event as a witness.
2. You were in a bank when you witnessed a robbery. Write your description of the event.
3. While coming home from work late last night you saw someone trying to set your neighbours' house on fire. Write your description of the event.

UNIT 8 Formal and Informal Letters/Emails

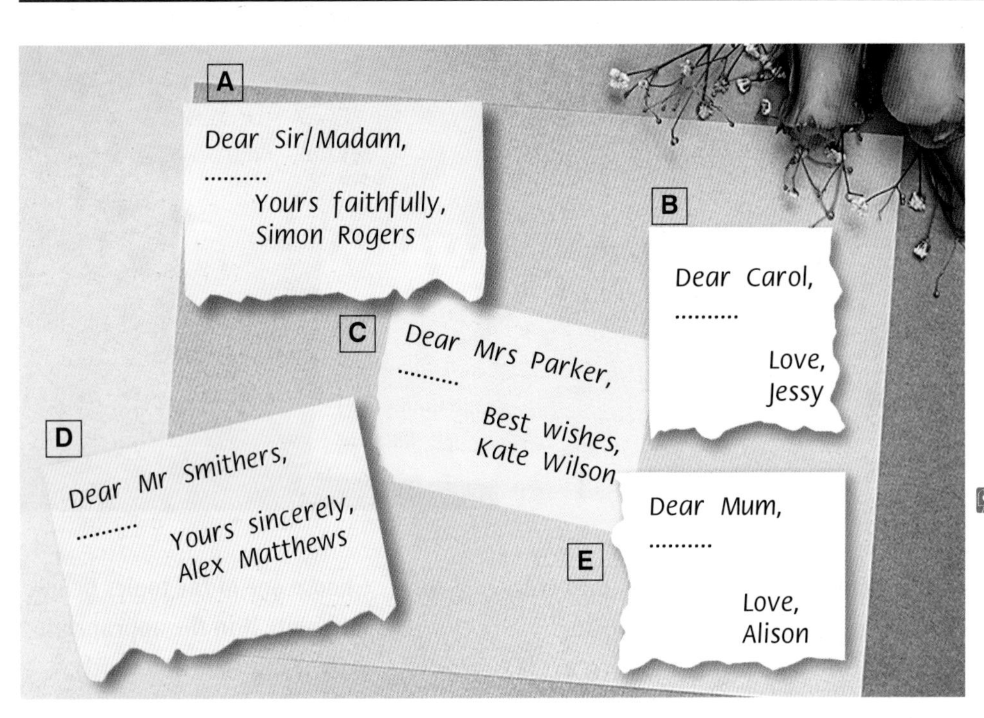

1 Look at the different layouts. Which are used to write a formal letter and which an informal letter? Which layout would you use to write a letter to a teacher? / a friend? / a company manager whose name you don't know?/ a company manager whose name you know?

2 Listen to four letters. Which letters are formal and which are informal? What is the reason for writing each letter? How does each letter begin and end?

There are various types of letters/emails such as: **letters/emails of complaint, letters/emails asking for/giving information, letters/emails of request, letters/emails asking for/giving advice, letters/emails of invitation, letters/emails accepting/refusing an invitation, letters/emails expressing congratulations/thanks/regret/sympathy, letters/emails giving news, letters/emails of apology, letters/emails of application for a job and letters/emails to the editor providing solutions/suggestions.**

A good letter/email should consist of:

a) **an appropriate greeting** *(Dear Peter, Dear Mr Ford, Dear Sir/ Madam,);*
b) **an introduction** clearly stating the reason you are writing;
c) **a main body** in which the subject is developed. Begin a new paragraph for each main point;
d) **a final paragraph** in which you sum up the topic or express your wish for something to be done ; and
e) **an appropriate ending** *(Yours/Best wishes, + first name, Yours sincerely,/Yours faithfully, + full name).*

Style in Letters/Emails

The characteristics of **formal style** in letters/emails are:

- the greeting (*Dear Mrs Lee, Dear Sir,)*
- frequent use of the passive
- formal language (complex sentences, non-colloquial English)
- no abbreviated forms
- the ending *(Yours sincerely,/Yours faithfully, Jason McNeil)*

The characteristics of **informal style** in letters/emails are:

- the greeting (*Dear Alex, Dear Dad,)*
- informal language and style (idioms, colloquial English)
- abbreviated forms, pronouns omitted
- the ending *(Yours/Love/Best wishes/Regards, Anthony)*

Note: When we write emails we usually separate paragraphs leaving a line blank in between each paragraph.

Introduction

Paragraph 1

reason(s) for writing

Main Body

Paragraph(s) 2 - 3

development of the subject

Conclusion

Final Paragraph

closing remarks

(full) name

Notes

- Informal (friendly) letters have only one address (yours) whereas formal letters have two (yours and the recipient's). Friendly letters/emails begin with **Dear + first name** and end with **Love / Yours / Best wishes + first name.** Formal letters/emails begin with a) **Dear Sir/Madam** and end with **Yours faithfully + full name** or b) **Dear Mr/Mrs + surname** and end with **Yours sincerely + full name.**
- Semi-formal letters/emails can begin with **Dear Mr/Mrs + surname** and end **Best wishes/ Yours + first name/full name**.

3 **Match the beginnings with the endings, then identify the type and style of each pair.**

BEGINNINGS...

1 I am writing with regard to your recent correspondence. We regret to inform you that there are no places left on the accountancy course ...

2 Thanks so much for your thoughtful gift. The jumper fits perfectly. It will really come in handy this winter when I go skiing ...

3 I just received your letter and I'm sorry to hear that you're having trouble ...

4 Sorry I can't make it to your parents' 25th anniversary party, but I'll be away on the day of the celebration.

5 I am writing to inquire about the special weekend trips ...

6 I am writing with regard to your advertisement in the *Daily News* of May 2nd. I would like to apply for the teaching position at Beacon Street School ...

7 I just wanted to let you know that I'd love to come to your party on the 24th.

8 It is with great pleasure that I am writing to congratulate you on your promotion.

...ENDINGS

A Anyway, wish them a happy anniversary from me. I'm looking forward to hearing about how it went.

B Let me know if my advice was of any help. I hope everything turns out fine.

C Should you need any information about courses which will be held next term, I would be happy to assist you.

D I look forward to meeting you to discuss the possibility of employment. Please contact me regarding any queries you may have.

E I look forward to receiving the information and would appreciate it if you could send it as soon as possible.

F Thanks again for the gift and please give my regards to your family.

G Anyway, thanks again for the invitation. I'll see you then.

H I am confident that you will carry out your new duties with your usual conscientiousness and dedication.

4 **Read the following sentences. Which are formal and which are informal? Which sentences are beginnings and which are endings of a letter/email? What kind of letter/email does each sentence belong to?**

1 We would be honoured if you could attend a reception for Ambassador Sarah Jacobs.

2 I can't wait to see you again, and don't forget to let me know if there's anything I should bring to the barbecue.

3 I am writing to inform you about some changes in the schedule for next term's courses.

4 We're organising a party and would be really glad if you could come.

5 Once again, I can't tell you how awful I feel about missing your birthday party.

6 I am writing to complain about the products I received from your company.

7 I look forward to receiving your advice on this matter.

8 Looking forward to seeing you and catching up on all your news.

9 Your thoughtful gift was greatly appreciated. Once again, thank you for your generosity.

10 I am very sorry but unfortunately you won't be able to use my summer house during the first week of August.

11 I'm so happy for you! Write back soon and tell me all about your new job.

12 Hope this advice helps.

a. Informal (Friendly) Letters/Emails - Giving News

1 **Read the following questions then listen to the dialogue and answer them.**
a) Why hasn't Steve written earlier?
b) What does he think of Hong Kong?
c) What is the weather like?
d) What happened to him recently?
e) What does he say about his new colleagues?
f) Is his new job easier than the one he had in London?
g) How does the writer feel about his new situation?

Informal (friendly) letters/emails are normally written to relatives, friends or other people we know very well. A good informal letter/email should be divided into paragraphs. Each paragraph should deal with one aspect of the subject and start with a topic sentence which gives the main idea of the paragraph.

Tenses

- Present Perfect and Past Simple are often used in letters/emails giving news. The Present Perfect is used to refer to recent activities and the Past Simple to refer to activities which happened at a stated time in the past.

Introduction

Paragraph 1
reason(s) for writing

Main Body

Paragraphs 2 - 3
development

Conclusion

Final Paragraph
closing remarks
first name

2 **Read the following letter and correct the mistakes. Write S for spelling, P for punctuation, WO for word order, G for grammar or WW for wrong word.**

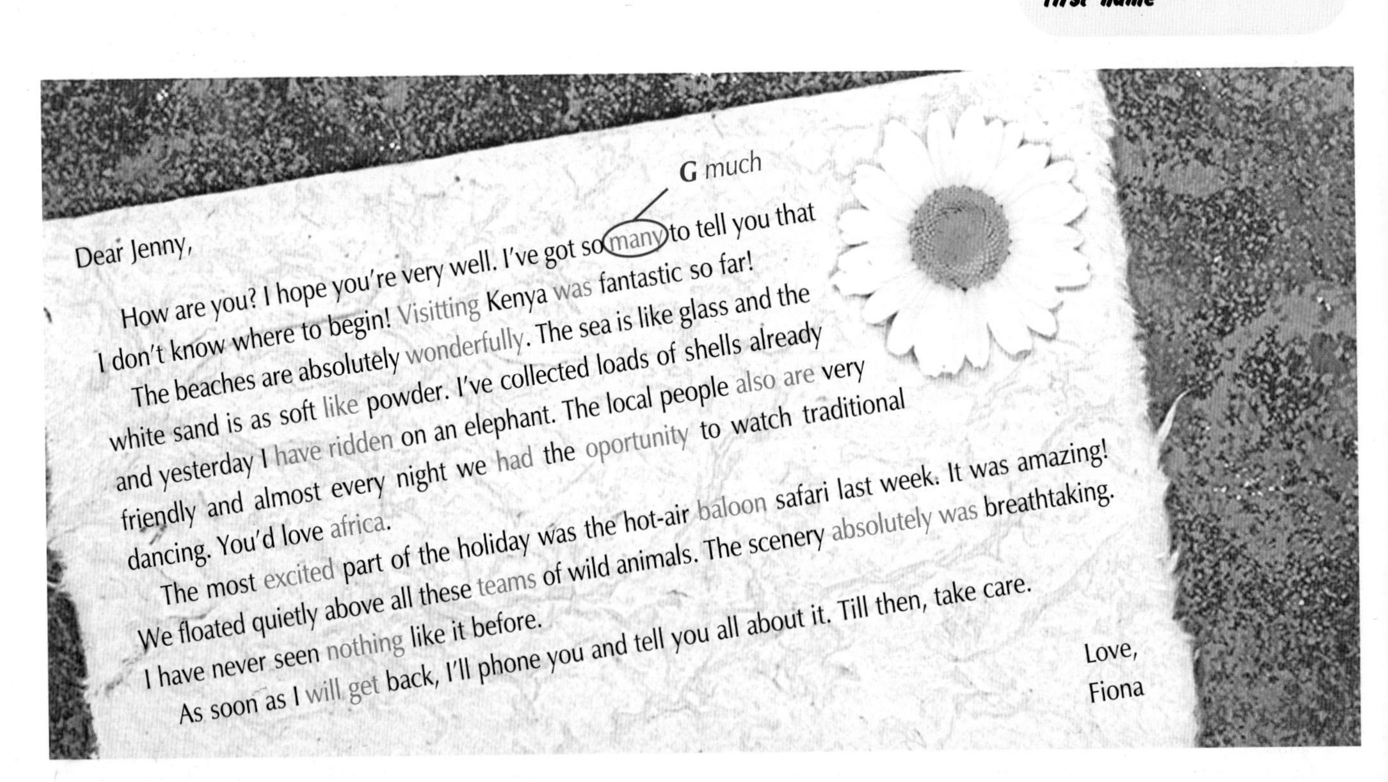

G much

Dear Jenny,

How are you? I hope you're very well. I've got so many to tell you that I don't know where to begin! Visitting Kenya was fantastic so far!

The beaches are absolutely wonderfully. The sea is like glass and the white sand is as soft like powder. I've collected loads of shells already and yesterday I have ridden on an elephant. The local people also are very friendly and almost every night we had the oportunity to watch traditional dancing. You'd love africa.

The most excited part of the holiday was the hot-air baloon safari last week. It was amazing! We floated quietly above all these teams of wild animals. The scenery absolutely was breathtaking. I have never seen nothing like it before.

As soon as I will get back, I'll phone you and tell you all about it. Till then, take care.

Love,
Fiona

3 Put the verbs in brackets into the Past Simple or the Present Perfect.

1 We .... (arrive) two days ago but we .... (not/see) any of the sights yet; so far we .... (spend) our time just relaxing.
2 I .... (be) so busy lately that I .... (not/have) time to do anything. I .... (go) out last night for the first time in weeks!
3 Bob .... (fly) to Rome yesterday. He .... (go) on a business trip and I really miss him; it's the first time we .... (be) apart since we .... (get) married.
4 We .... (sell) the house last month but we .... (not/move) into our new house yet. The builders still .... (not/finish) the bathroom, even though they .... (start) work on it three months ago.

4 Read the email below and put the verbs in brackets into the correct tense. What is being described in this email?

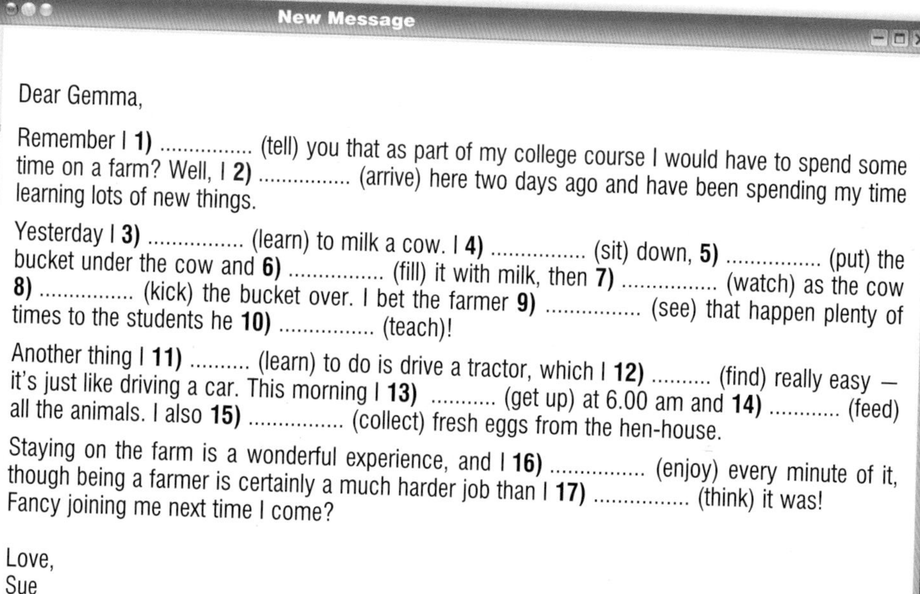

New Message

Dear Gemma,

Remember I **1)** .... (tell) you that as part of my college course I would have to spend some time on a farm? Well, I **2)** .... (arrive) here two days ago and have been spending my time learning lots of new things.

Yesterday I **3)** .... (learn) to milk a cow. I **4)** .... (sit) down, **5)** .... (put) the bucket under the cow and **6)** .... (fill) it with milk, then **7)** .... (watch) as the cow **8)** .... (kick) the bucket over. I bet the farmer **9)** .... (see) that happen plenty of times to the students he **10)** .... (teach)!

Another thing I **11)** .... (learn) to do is drive a tractor, which I **12)** .... (find) really easy – it's just like driving a car. This morning I **13)** .... (get up) at 6.00 am and **14)** .... (feed) all the animals. I also **15)** .... (collect) fresh eggs from the hen-house.

Staying on the farm is a wonderful experience, and I **16)** .... (enjoy) every minute of it, though being a farmer is certainly a much harder job than I **17)** .... (think) it was! Fancy joining me next time I come?

Love,
Sue

5 Read the following letter and replace the underlined formal phrases with more appropriate informal ones.

Dear Mum,

I felt obliged to write to inform you how everything is going here in Spain since I started university. Please accept my sincere apologies for not writing sooner but I've been so busy I really haven't had a suitable opportunity.

I managed to find a nice place to live. It's a small flat just around the corner from the university. I'm sharing the flat with a girl called Anita who seems really nice and has been here for a year.

I have become familiar with my surroundings and have been practising my Spanish, which is improving considerably every day.

I hope to return home for Christmas once the examinations are over. It will be wonderful to see everyone again. I do get homesick, you know.

I look forward to hearing from you soon.

Yours sincerely,
Julie

6 Write the following in the appropriate style using 120 – 180 words.

1 Last week your colleagues at the office threw a surprise party to celebrate your promotion. Write a letter to a friend telling him/her about the party.
2 You have been on holiday abroad for a week. Write an email to your parents describing your holiday so far.

b. Asking for/Giving Advice

1 A. Read the following questions, then listen to the dialogue and answer them. You may take notes while listening.

a) Who did Pat send a letter to?
b) Is the letter formal or informal?
c) What is the reason for writing?
d) What problems does she describe in the letter?
e) How does Pat start and finish the letter?

B. Read the following questions, then listen to the second letter and answer them.

a) What is the reason for writing?
b) What advice is given?
c) How does the letter start and end?
d) Is it an informal, formal or semi-formal letter?

2 Look at the two plans in the right-hand column of this page. Which plan was followed in each letter?

Letters/Emails asking for or giving advice can be formal, informal or semi-formal depending on the situation. A letter/An email **asking for advice** can be sent to a friend, a consultant or an advice column in a magazine. Details of the problem should be mentioned. A letter/An email **giving advice** should contain suggestions introduced with appropriate language.

Useful Language for Letters/Emails Asking for Advice

- **Opening Remarks**: (Formal) I am writing to ask if you could help me with / I would appreciate it if you could give me some advice about / I am writing to ask for your advice / I would be grateful if you could offer your advice / Could you possibly offer your advice / I wonder if you could help me with a problem, etc. (Informal) I'm writing to ask for your advice / Can you give me your advice / I've got a problem and I need your advice, etc.
- **Closing Remarks**: (Formal) I would appreciate it if you could give me your advice as soon as possible / I look forward to receiving your advice / It would be of great help if you could advise me, etc. (Informal) What do you think I should do? / Please let me know what you think I should do. / Please tell me what to do, etc.

Useful Language for Letters/Emails Giving Advice

- **Opening Remarks**: (Formal) Thank you for your letter/email requesting / I am writing in reply to your letter asking for advice about / I hope the following advice will be of some help to you, etc. (Informal) I just got your letter and I think I can help you / I was sorry to hear about your problem. Here's what I think you should do, etc.
- **Suggestions** can be introduced with expressions such as: (Formal) I strongly recommend that / I would suggest that / I believe the best course of action is / I would advise you to / You should / You ought to / If I were you I would (Informal) Why don't you / You should / You ought to / It would be a good idea to / What you should do is ... / How about ... / I think you should ... / The best advice I can give you is..., etc.
- **Closing Remarks**: (Formal) I trust you will accept this advice / I hope this will be of help / I would very much like to know if this was helpful (Informal) Hope this has helped / Let me know what happens, etc.

Asking for advice

Introduction

Paragraph 1

reason(s) for writing

Main Body

Paragraphs 2 - 3

description of problem(s)

Conclusion

Final Paragraph

closing remarks

(full) name

Giving advice

Introduction

Paragraph 1

thanks for letter/express understanding of problem

Main Body

Paragraphs 2 - 3

suggestion(s) + reason(s)

Conclusion

Final Paragraph

closing remarks

(full) name

3 **Read the following letters and answer these questions. What kind of letters are they? Which letter is formal and which is informal? What is the topic of each paragraph in each letter? Now replace the underlined phrases with other similar expressions, keeping the appropriate style.**

MODEL A

Dear Miss Pierson,

Thank you for your letter asking for my advice about what you should do now that you have finished school. I realise how difficult this stage must be for you, but there are a range of options for you to choose from.

If I were you, I would make a list of all the careers which may interest you and then decide which one you feel you are best suited to in terms of exam grades or subject interest. I would also suggest that you see a careers officer who would be able to give you professional advice. Furthermore, it would be a good idea to write to some universities and ask them to send you a prospectus; you may find a course which really appeals to you.

I hope these suggestions will be of help to you. I wish you well in whatever course of action you decide upon. Do let me know what you decide to do; it is always good to hear from former pupils.

Yours sincerely,
Linda Steel

MODEL B

Dear Stephanie,

Thanks for your letter asking me for advice about how to lose weight. I was sorry to hear that you're feeling depressed. I'm sure your problem isn't as serious as you say it is. You always did exaggerate!

The best advice I can give you is to choose one diet and really stick to it for a couple of months; it's pointless trying lots of different ones which only last a few days, as you've discovered! If I were you, I would go on the same diet I went on: I've sent you the information booklet. The most important thing to remember is to eat plenty of fruit and vegetables and to exercise regularly.

Why don't you join the basketball team? I know how much you love basketball. Also, once you start losing weight you should give yourself little rewards, like a visit to the hairdresser or a new dress. That way you'll probably find that you won't think about food so much.

If you follow my advice, I'm sure you'll be back in shape in no time. Anyway, let me know how it goes.

Lots of love,
Kate

4 **Study the following situations and, using appropriate expressions, offer advice to each person.**

1 Your friend wants some advice on what she should take with her on her first trip abroad.
2 Your boyfriend/girlfriend has asked you for advice on how to impress your parents the first time he/she meets them.
3 A colleague at work has asked you to advise him how to gain a promotion.
4 You are a doctor and a patient needs advice on how he can successfully lower his high cholesterol level.
5 Your brother would like some advice about what to look out for when buying a second-hand car.

5 **Write the following in the appropriate style using 120 - 180 words.**

1 Your parents will not let you go on holiday as they want you to study for your exams. Write a letter to a friend asking for his/her advice on this matter.
2 The extract below is part of an email you received recently from a friend. Write a reply giving her some advice about what she should do.

"I failed all my A-level exams so now I can't get into university. I feel like such a failure; I'll never get a degree now."

3 You feel that you and your mother cannot agree on anything. Write a letter to a problem page asking for advice.

C. Letters/Emails of Complaint

1 **Read the table below, then listen to the cassette and fill in the missing information. What complaints did the client make? Why? What action did she ask to be taken?**

	Complaint	Justification (but I had been told that ...)
a)	I stayed in a huge multi-storey	I would be staying in a family-run .... house.
b)	The resort was .... with tourists.	The resort was .... and unspoilt.
c)	The beach was a .... bus ride away.	The beach was a .... walk away.

- Letters/Emails of complaint are normally written in a formal style.
- Mild or strong language can be used depending on the feelings of the writer or the seriousness of the complaint, but abusive language must never be used.
  e.g. **Mild Complaint:** *I am writing to complain about a damaged videotape I bought at your shop.*
  I hope you will deal with this matter/resolve this matter quickly.
  Strong Complaint: *I am writing to express my disgust at the appalling treatment I received while staying at your hotel.*
  I insist upon full compensation or I will be forced to take this matter further.
- Start a new paragraph for each different aspect of the topic.
- You should state the reason for the complaint in the first paragraph.
- Any complaints you make should be supported with a justification.
- Complaints and justification can be linked together as follows:
  I still haven't received the goods I ordered ***in spite of/despite the fact that*** *I sent you a cheque three weeks ago.*
  Although/Even though *I have only used the automatic tin-opener once, it no longer works. I have written to you twice* ***but*** *you have not taken any action.*
  I have already written to you twice. ***Nevertheless,/However,*** *you have not taken any action.*

Introduction

Paragraph 1

reason for writing

Main Body

Paragraphs 2 - 3

complaint(s) and justification

Conclusion

Final Paragraph

suggested action to be taken, closing remarks

full name

2 **Match the complaints with the justification using appropriate linking words.**

Complaint

1. My 2-year-old daughter cut herself on the toy.
2. When we received the bill we realised we had been charged the full price.
3. The top rack of the dishwasher has broken.
4. You still keep delivering equipment to the wrong address.
5. I received a letter saying my licence has expired.
6. The shirt's bright red collar has turned pink.
7. I had to share a bathroom with other guests.

Justification

a) I sent you a cheque to renew it a month ago.
b) I informed you of my change of business address.
c) I booked a room with a private bathroom.
d) I have only used it three times.
e) You claim it is safe for children over 18 months.
f) The label states that it can be washed at high temperatures without the colours fading.
g) We were told there would be a 20% discount if we ordered before June.

Useful Language for Letters/Emails of Complaint

Opening Remarks: (Mild) I am writing to complain about/regarding/on account of/because of/on the subject of .../I am writing to draw your attention to .../I am writing to you in connection with ... etc. (Strong) I was appalled at/I want to express my strong dissatisfaction with/I feel I must protest/complain about, etc.
Closing Remarks: (Mild) I hope/assume you will replace/I trust the situation will improve/I hope the matter will be resolved/I hope we can sort this matter out amicably, etc.
(Strong) I insist you replace the item at once/I demand a full refund/I hope that I will not be forced to take further action, etc.

3 **Read the letter and state the topic of each paragraph. Is it a mild or strong letter of complaint? Then fill in the table below with the complaints and the justification.**

Subject	To/From	Date	Priority

Dear Sir/Madam,

I want to express my strong dissatisfaction with the service I received during a visit to your restaurant on December 12th. Firstly, I had booked a table for my wife and myself for 8:30, but it was 9 o'clock before we were seated. Such a delay seems to me inexcusable.

Then, in spite of the fact that I had repeated our order to check that the waiter had heard me correctly, he proceeded to bring us the wrong starters. Such careless service should not be tolerated in a restaurant which charges such high prices.

To make matters worse, the chocolate gateau we were served for dessert was quite stale. The menu claimed, though, that all desserts were freshly prepared that day.

My wife and I will not be dining in your restaurant again; however, as manager, you would be wise to guard against such appalling treatment of your customers in future.

Yours faithfully,
Larry Dunman

Complaints	Justification

4 **Read the following letter and correct the mistakes. Write S for spelling, G for grammar, P for punctuation, WO for word order or WW for wrong word.**

Dear Sir/Madam, G am writing

I wrote to complain for a washing machine who I recently took from your company.

When I used the machine for the first time properly it worked and the clothes come out clean and fresh. Also, when I used the machine the second time, it seemed to have been a malfunction while the rinse cycle. The clothes still had quite a lot of soap in them when I have taken them out.

Furthermore, when I tryed washing another load of laundry the same thing happened. In addition to this, the machine did not hit the water to the right temperature. Even though I had turned the dial to 50°C, the water in the machine remained cold throughout the entire cycle.

i assume you will replace the washing machine as it is obviously wrong. I hope the matter will resolve promptly.

Yours faithfuly,
nancy Gillis

When you want to introduce another complaint in a letter/an email, you can begin the sentence with one of the following linking words or phrases: **what is more, in addition, furthermore, moreover,** etc.

5 Punctuate the following email of complaint and divide it into paragraphs. Then comment on the tone of this email.

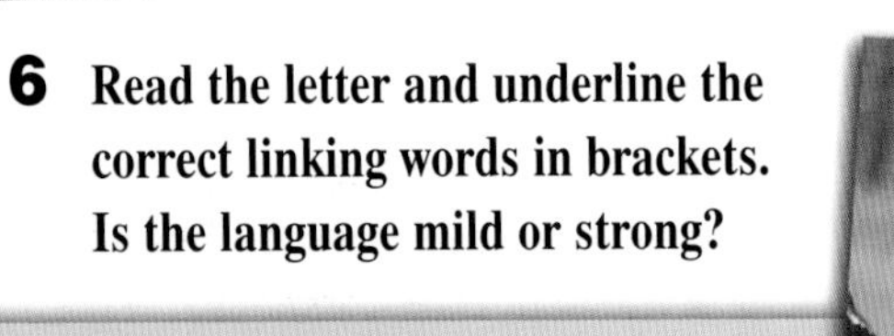

New Message

Dear Mr Haynes

i am writing to complain about the two alsatian dogs that you own although i have repeatedly asked you to prevent the dogs from leaving your garden you have failed to do so as a result my front lawn has been dug up twice over the past three days furthermore their continual barking is extremely disruptive both to local residents and myself finally I feel that these dogs have a tendency to be aggressive as I have told you in the past nevertheless they are allowed to roam the streets of our neighbourhood which I consider unacceptable i hope that having made my feelings clear to you this matter can be resolved

Yours sincerely,
William Penton

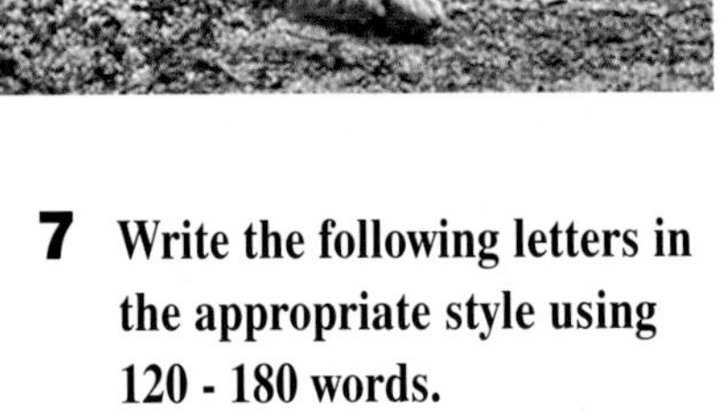

6 Read the letter and underline the correct linking words in brackets. Is the language mild or strong?

Dear Mrs Brosnan,

I am writing to complain about a waterproof jacket I purchased from your shop last week.

1) (However/Although) the jacket was supposed to be completely waterproof, I got soaked the first time I wore it in wet weather. **2) (Furthermore/But)**, when I tried to take the jacket off, the zip wouldn't open and when I tried to get it unstuck, the jacket tore.

I sent the jacket back to your shop after having been assured by one of the assistants that I would be sent a refund. **3) (However /In addition)**, I still have not received one.

As a regular customer of yours, I feel disappointed with the way I have been treated and hope that steps will be taken to rectify the situation.

I trust this matter will receive your immediate attention.

Yours sincerely,
John Wells

7 Write the following letters in the appropriate style using 120 - 180 words.

1 You stayed at a holiday resort recommended by your travel agent. However, you did not enjoy your stay due to a number of difficulties. Write an email describing them and asking for action to be taken.

2 You have recently bought a cassette player but it does not work properly. Write a letter of complaint to the manager of the shop where you bought it.

d. Letters/Emails of Apology

1 **Read the following questions, then listen to the cassette and answer them. You may take notes while listening.**
a) Why has Dave written a letter?
b) What reasons does he give?
c) How does Dave's letter end?
d) Is Dave's letter formal or informal?

A letter/An email of apology can be either formal or informal. It can be written when someone has made a mistake, has failed to perform a duty or is not able to fulfil a promise. The main body contains reasons for the inconvenience caused. In the final paragraph you can express your hope to improve the situation or promise to make up for any problems that have been caused.

2 **Read the email below and divide it into paragraphs. Then read it again and answer the following questions: a) Why was the letter written? b) What reason is given for the inconvenience? c) What action will be taken to make up for the inconvenience caused? d) What style of language has been used? e) What is the topic of each paragraph?**

Sunrise Travel Agency
25 Baker Street, London Tel: + 41222345 Fax: + 41583796

Dear Mrs Brown,

On behalf of Sunrise Travel, please accept my sincere apologies for your dissatisfaction with your Caribbean holiday in February. Due to a computer error we were forced to change your accommodation at the last minute to what we had been led to believe was a hotel of equally high standard. Sadly, it was not until later that we discovered the hotel in question did not meet the requirements demanded of Sunrise Travel accommodation. As a long established travel company, we are well aware of the upset that can be caused by problems experienced while on holiday. For this reason we would like to offer you a weekend for two in Paris at a top-class hotel as compensation. Once again, our sincerest apologies for the inconvenience caused. We look forward to hearing from you.

Yours sincerely,
John Greenway

Introduction

Paragraph 1
reason for writing

Main Body

Paragraphs 2 - 3
reasons to explain the inconvenience caused

Conclusion

Final Paragraph
express understanding/regret or promise to make up for the situation

closing remarks
full name

Useful Language for Letters/Emails of Apology

Opening Remarks: (Formal) I am writing to apologise for/I must apologise for/Please accept my sincerest apologies for/How can I apologise enough for/I must apologise profusely for, etc. (Informal) I hope you will understand when I say that/What can I say, except I'm sorry that/I'm sorry for/ I owe you an apology/I'm so sorry if I upset you in any way/ I can't describe how sorry I am and how guilty I feel, etc.

Closing Remarks: (Formal) Once again, sincerest apologies for/I hope you will accept my apologies/I hope my apologies will be/are accepted, etc. (Informal) I hope you believe me when I say how sorry I am/I can't tell you how sorry I am/ I beg you to forgive me for/There is no excuse for ... and I hope you'll forgive me, etc.

3 **Read the two letters below and fill in the gaps with expressions from the list. Then answer the following questions: a) Which letter is formal and which informal? b) What is the reason for writing each letter? c) What is the topic of the final paragraph in these two letters? d) What complaint had been made in each situation? Finally, underline the opening and closing remarks then replace them with others from the table above.**

1 to apologise/ to say how sorry I am
2 bad behaviour/disgraceful conduct
3 I know/I realise
4 sort out the problem/resolve the matter
5 Due to my absence/Because I wasn't there
6 but/However
7 severely reprimanded/properly told off
8 be sure/rest assured
9 what happened/this incident
10 put you off/deter you

A

Dear Mr Johnson,
I am writing to you **1)** .... for the **2)** .... of a member of our staff towards you on Saturday April 23rd. **3)** .... how much this must have upset you, and I hope that we can **4)** .... agreeably.

5) .... at the time, I was unable to apologise to you in person. **6)** ...., I always take such incidents extremely seriously and, following your letter of complaint, the member of staff has been **7)** .... You can **8)** .... that he will be treating our customers quite differently in future.

I hope that **9)** .... will not **10)** .... from using our store in future. In an attempt to make up for the inconvenience caused, we are sending you a complimentary gift.

Yours sincerely,
Peter Brown (Manager)

B

Dear Belinda,
I'm writing **1)** .... for my son's **2)** .... last week. **3)** .... how upset you were, and I thought I'd write to you to try and **4)** ....

5) .... when you called round, I didn't realise what had happened straight away, **6)** .... when I got your letter, I promise you that he got **7)** .... You can **8)** .... he'll never speak to you like that again.

I hope **9)** .... won't **10)** .... coming round to our house again. I'd like to make up for my son's behaviour by inviting you to dinner on Thursday so that he can have the chance to say how sorry he is himself.

Love,
Joanne

4 **Write the following in the appropriate style using 120 - 180 words.**

1 You have promised your boss that you will work some extra hours next weekend. Due to a family problem, you will be unable to fulfil your promise. Write a letter of apology to your boss explaining your reasons and promising to make it up to him/her.

2 Your friend let you spend the weekend at his seaside cottage. While staying there you accidentally stained an expensive Persian rug. Write an email apologising for the damage and offering to get it cleaned.

e. Letters/Emails of Invitation

1 **Read the following questions, then listen and answer them. You may take notes while listening.**

a) What is the purpose of the letter?
b) How does the letter begin and end?
c) Is it formal or informal?

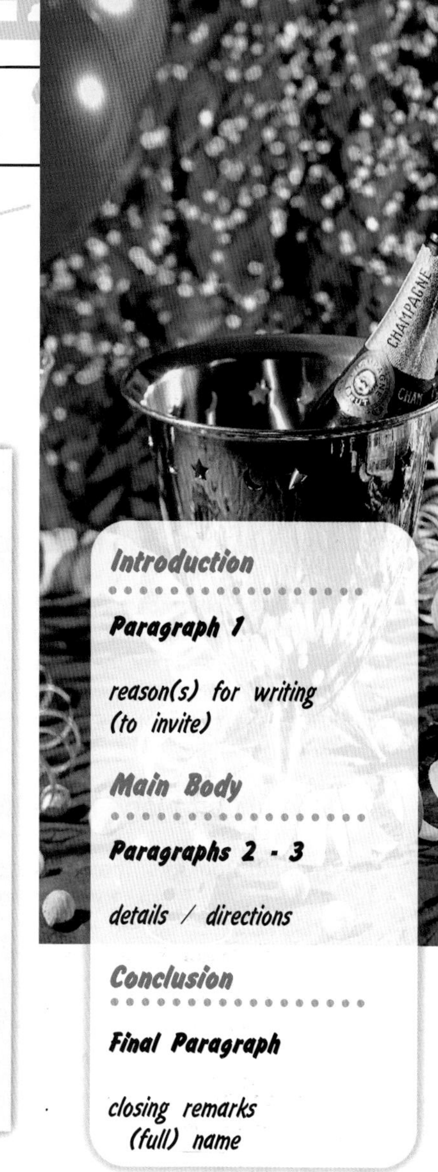

- Letters/Emails of invitation can be formal or informal depending on the situation and who we are writing to. They usually contain some additional information, for example: latest news, description of the event (party, wedding, etc.) place (hotel, house, etc.) and/or directions to the place.

Useful Language for Letters/Emails of Invitation

Opening Remarks: (Formal) We would be honoured if you / I cordially invite you to / Your presence would be appreciated at / You are invited to attend, etc. (Informal) I'm writing to invite you to .../ I'd love it if you could come to / We're organising a ... and would love it if you could come, etc.
Closing Remarks: (Formal) We would be grateful if you could / Please indicate whether you will be able to attend, etc. (Informal) I hope you'll be able to make it / Hope you can come / Looking forward to seeing you then / Please let me know as soon as possible, etc.

- **Directions** can be introduced by using some of the following expressions: In case you don't know the way, I'll give you some directions / I have included some directions / Here are a few directions so you don't get lost / In case you do not know the exact location of the ..., etc.

2 **Read the letter below and answer the following questions. Who is going to read this letter? Is it formal or informal? What is the topic of each paragraph? Read the letter again and underline the opening and closing remarks, then replace them with other appropriate expressions.**

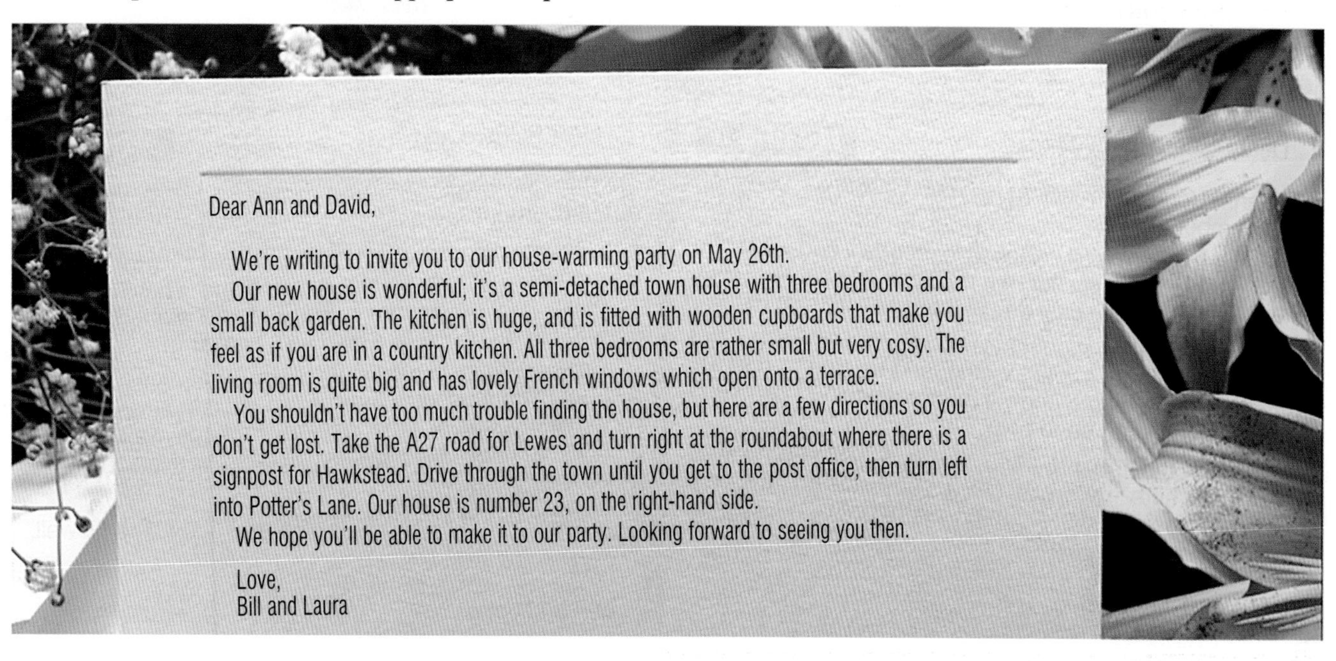

Dear Ann and David,

We're writing to invite you to our house-warming party on May 26th.

Our new house is wonderful; it's a semi-detached town house with three bedrooms and a small back garden. The kitchen is huge, and is fitted with wooden cupboards that make you feel as if you are in a country kitchen. All three bedrooms are rather small but very cosy. The living room is quite big and has lovely French windows which open onto a terrace.

You shouldn't have too much trouble finding the house, but here are a few directions so you don't get lost. Take the A27 road for Lewes and turn right at the roundabout where there is a signpost for Hawkstead. Drive through the town until you get to the post office, then turn left into Potter's Lane. Our house is number 23, on the right-hand side.

We hope you'll be able to make it to our party. Looking forward to seeing you then.

Love,
Bill and Laura

Letters/Emails accepting/refusing an invitation can be formal or informal. In letters/emails accepting an invitation, we begin by expressing thanks for the invitation. Further comments can be included such as asking the person whether there is anything we can do, or asking for more information concerning the invitation.

In letters/emails refusing an invitation, we begin by expressing thanks for the invitation, and we go on to give reasons why we are unable to accept it.

Useful Language for Letters/Emails Accepting an Invitation

Opening Remarks: (Formal) I am writing to thank you for the kind invitation/ Thank you for the kind invitation which I would be honoured to accept, etc. (Informal) Thanks for the invitation to ..., ... sounds lovely ..., etc.
Closing Remarks: (Formal) I look forward to seeing you / We await the event with great anticipation, etc. (Informal) See you then/ We're really looking forward to it, etc.

Useful Language for Letters/Emails Refusing an Invitation

Opening Remarks: (Formal) We thank you for your recent invitation to ... but etc. (Informal) Thanks for the invitation, but/ Thanks for inviting me to ..., but I'm afraid I can't come, etc.
Closing Remarks: (Formal) I am sorry to miss the opportunity of/ Thank you again for the invitation / I hope we will have the opportunity to meet, etc. (Informal) I hope we can get together some other time / I'm really sorry we'll have to miss it, etc.

Accepting an Invitation

Introduction

Paragraph 1
thanks for invitation

Main Body

Paragraphs 2 - 3
acceptance of invitation, further comments

Conclusion

Final Paragraph
closing remarks
(full) name

Refusing an Invitation

Introduction

Paragraph 1
thanks for invitation

Main Body

Paragraphs 2 - 3
refusal of invitation, giving reasons

Conclusion

Final Paragraph
closing remarks
(full) name

3 **Read the emails below and answer the following questions. a) What kind of emails are they? b) What style is used in each? c) What is the topic of each paragraph in these emails? Read the emails again and underline the opening and closing remarks, then replace them with other appropriate expressions.**

Subject | To/From | Date | Priority

MODEL A

Dear Richard and Judy,

Thanks for the invitation to your Christmas party on December 18th.

John and I were really pleased to receive it and we'd love to come. It's lucky for us that you chose the 18th, actually, as it's the only day of that week that we're free.

It's been such a long time since we've seen each other so it will be great to get together and catch up on all the news. Please let me know if there's anything I can bring or anything I can do to help.

Oh, one other thing. Will it be all right to bring Samantha? I 'm not sure if we can get a babysitter on that day. Thanks again, and see you on the 18th.

Love,
Ann and John

Subject | To/From | Date | Priority

MODEL B

Dear Richard and Judy,

The Christmas party you invited us to on December 18th sounds lovely.

Unfortunately, we won't be able to make it as it is John's mother's birthday on that day and she is having a small family party to celebrate. She's almost eighty years old and still as strong as ever – it's amazing!

It's such a pity because we haven't seen each other for ages. You must give us a call so we can arrange to get together another time instead. Perhaps we'll throw a party on New Year's Eve so we can see everyone. We'll let you know.

Thanks for the invitation, and hope the party goes well.

Love,
Ann and John

4 **Complete the sentences by replacing the symbols with an appropriate word or phrase.**

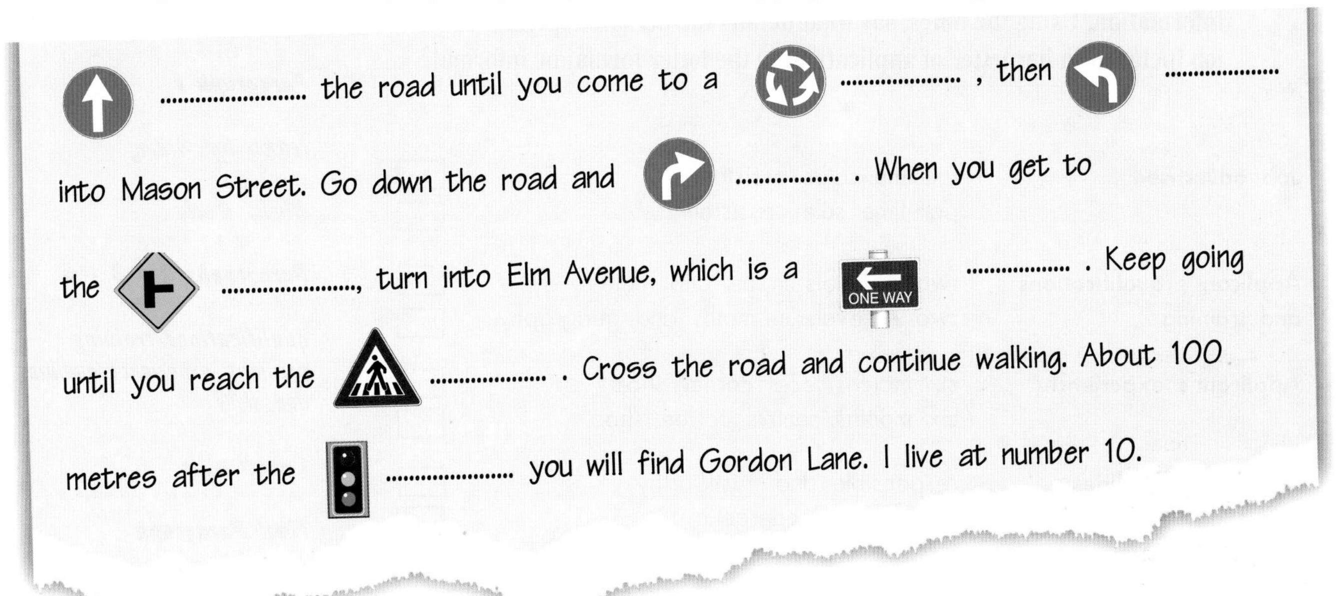

5 **Match the beginnings with the endings, then identify the style and type of letters they belong to.**

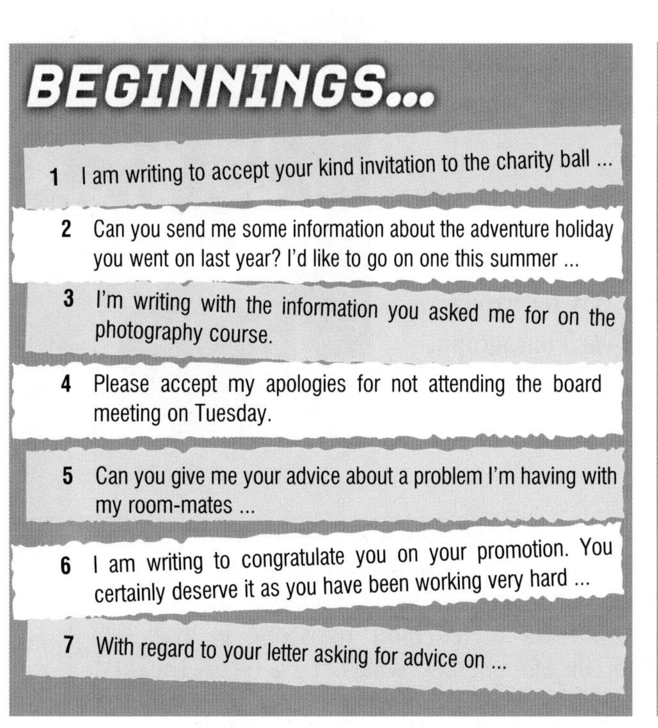

...ENDINGS

a ... Let me know if you need any more information about other photography courses because I've attended quite a few.

b ... I hope that this advice will prove useful. Please let me know what you decide to do.

c ... Once again, thank you for the invitation.

d ... Your advice would help me a lot. I know you've had similar problems and I'd like to know how you solved them.

e ... Please, send the details soon because I'm trying to plan my holiday and I can't decide where to go.

f ... I hope you will accept my apologies. Perhaps we can meet on Friday to discuss the board's plans.

g ... I am confident that you will be successful in your new position. I wish you every success in your career.

6 **Write the following in the appropriate style using 120 – 180 words.**

1 You have received an invitation to a birthday party from your cousin. Write an email accepting the invitation and suggesting that you organise the music.

2 The head of your firm and his wife are celebrating their 25th wedding anniversary and have invited you to the event. Write a letter thanking them for the invitation and saying why you will be unable to attend.

f. Letters/Emails of Application

1 **Read the following table, then listen to the cassette and tick the correct information. Using the notes, say what details the person applying for the job included in her letter of application. Is the letter formal or informal?**

Job advertised	full-time sales assistant	☐
	part-time sales assistant	☐
Applicant's qualifications and training	two A levels in art and maths	☐
	two A levels in maths and geography	☐
Applicant's experience	six months/local corner shop	☐
	six months/central coffee shop	☐
Applicant's qualities and skills	responsible and trustworthy	☐
	decisive and energetic	☐
Applicant's additional information and reference	enclosed CV/available for interview	☐
	enclosed a photo/available for interview	☐

Introduction

Paragraph 1

reason for writing

Main Body

Paragraphs 2 - 3 - 4

qualifications/training – previous experience/qualities and skills

Conclusion

Final Paragraph

closing remarks
full name

A letter/An email of application may be written when we apply for a permanent/temporary job or educational course. It is usually formal; therefore, the appropriate language and expressions should be used.

2 **Read the following letter and correct the mistakes. Write S for spelling, G for grammar, P for punctuation, WO for word order or WW for wrong word. Read the letter again and write down the topic of each paragraph.**

Dear Sir/Madam, *S writing*

I am writting to apply for the place of Physical Education teacher at the All Saints' Girls' school in Liverpool as advertising in *The Herald* of 24th May.

I am twenty-six year old and obtained a degree in Sports Science at liverpool University at 1991. I am presently worked as a teaching assistant in the P.E. department at highfield Grammar School in Manchester where I was for the last four years. Prior to this, I wasted two years as a swimming coach in Middlesex at the Regent Leisure Centre.

I am interested extremely in the post available as I am eager to upgrade my present status from teaching assistant to fuly appointed P.E. teacher. I am patient and believe in encouraging the all pupils to reach their full potential.

If you wish me to atend an interview, I shall be glad to do so.
I am looking forward to hear from you.

Yours faithfully,
Barbara Winters

Useful Language for Letters/Emails of Application (for a Job)

Opening Remarks: I am writing with regard to your advertisement/ I am writing to apply for the post / job / position of/which I saw advertised in ..., etc.
Reference to experience: ... for the last/past year I have been working as ... since / for ... / I have had experience of ... / Two years ago I was employed as ... / I worked as ... before ..., etc.
Closing Remarks: I would appreciate a reply at your earliest convenience / Please contact me regarding any queries you may have / I enclose my CV and I would be glad to attend an interview at any time convenient to you / I look forward to hearing from you in due course, etc.

3 **Read the CV and the email. Then, say which information given in the CV has not been included in the email. Finally, suggest alternative beginnings and endings.**

Name:	Miranda Beeton (single)
Address:	15 Oak Tree Drive, Southampton
Date of Birth:	28 October 1974
Education:	1985 - 1992: Tolworth Secondary School GCSE's: Maths, Geography, English, Computing, History, French, Spanish A levels: French, Spanish, History 1992 - 1995: B.A., Tourism Studies - University of East London
Work Experience:	June - September 1995 — Travel Agent, Sky High Tourist Agency October 1995 - Present — European Tour Guide, Sunshine Tours
Other Information:	Computer skills: Certificate of Proficiency in word-processing and graphics Languages spoken: French, Spanish, some German Interests: tennis, travelling , reading
Referees:	J. G. Malcom (President) Sky High Tourist Agency *25, Midtown Street, Southampton* B. Needham (Manager) Sunshine Tours *1,Hortanza Calle,Madrid, Spain*

Dear Sir/Madam,

I am writing to apply for the position of Senior Tour Guide which was advertised in Monday's edition of *The Evening News*.

I graduated from the University of East London in 1995 with a degree in Tourism Studies. I have been working as a European Tour Guide since 1995 for Sunshine Tours, which is based in Spain. Prior to this, I worked as a Travel Agent for Sky High Tourist Agency during the summer season. I hold certificates in computer graphics and word-processing. I speak fluent French and Spanish and some German.

I am friendly, organised and patient and work well under pressure. As my references show, I have been very popular with many of the clients who specifically asked for me to be their tour-guide on tours they went on.

I have enclosed a copy of my CV. I would be glad to attend an interview at any time convenient to you.

Yours faithfully,
Miranda Beeton

4 **Match the qualities with the professions. Some qualities can be used more than once. Then make sentences as in the example.**

patient, alert, skilful, open-minded, dedicated, organised, approachable, understanding, calm, imaginative, logical, creative, knowledgeable, kind, confident, able to cope in a crisis, good communication skills, able to work under pressure, sense of humour, polite, conscientious, tolerant

teacher

pharmacist

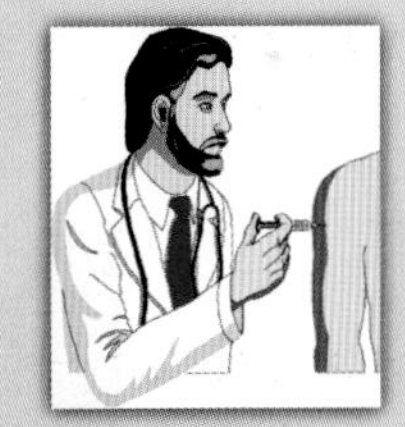
doctor

reporter

waitress

computer programmer

chef

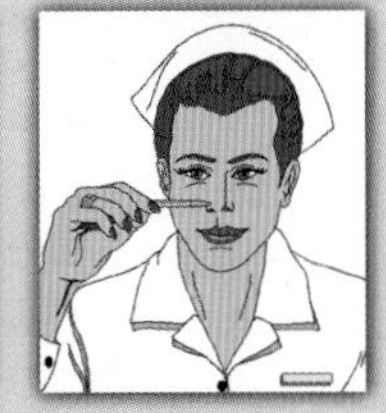
nurse

e.g. A teacher has to be patient because children need time to learn certain things.

Useful Language for Letters/Emails of Application (for a Course)

Opening Remarks: I would like to apply for admission to the ... beginning/I would like to be considered for, etc.
Reference to experience: I hold a certificate/ degree in/ I am due to take examinations in/ I have taken/passed the ... examination/ I hold the following qualification / I have completed the following courses/degree course/My degree is in English, etc.
Closing Remarks: I would appreciate a reply at your earliest convenience / I look forward to meeting / hearing from you/Please contact me regarding any queries you may have / I enclose further details of my education and qualifications to date / I hope that you will consider me for entry / I look forward to receiving your response in the near future, etc.

5 **Read the letter below and underline the formal expressions. Then replace them with similar expressions from the table above. Finally, give the topic of each paragraph and say what kind of letter it is.**

Dear Sir/Madam,

I am writing to apply for a place on the Archaeology MA course which commences this September at Macbriney University.

I am 25 years old and I have completed a Bachelor´s degree in Archaeology at Drakeham University, where I received first class honours. Prior to this I was a pupil at Berkeley Comprehensive, where I obtained 9 GCSEs and three A levels in History, Geography and Latin.

Since the completion of my BA I have spent two years working as assistant archaeologist on a site in Egypt. During this expedition I have assisted in the discovery of several interesting artifacts. This work was extremely enjoyable and I am now anxious to specialise by gaining further qualifications before embarking on my chosen career in this field.

I enclose a detailed curriculum vitae in the hope that you will consider my application for entry. I look forward to receiving your response in the near future.

Yours faithfully,
Jill Holland

Applying for a Course

Introduction

Paragraph 1

reason for writing

Main Body

Paragraphs 2 - 3

qualifications / reasons for wanting to take the course

Conclusion

Final Paragraph

closing remarks
full name

6 **Write the following in the appropriate style using 120 - 180 words.**

1 You want to go to Winston University to do a degree in History. Write a letter applying for a place on the course.

2 You have decided to spend some time working this summer. You have seen an advertisement in the paper for lifeguards to work for a month on one of the most popular beaches in Sussex. Write an email asking to be considered for one of the positions.

UNIT 9 Transactional Letters/Emails

- Transactional letters/emails are letters/emails which respond to writing input (advertisements, other letters, emails, notes, invitations, etc) and/or visual prompts (maps, drawings, etc).
  They can either be formal or informal, depending on who you are writing to.
- Transactional letters/emails can be of any type (complaint, application, invitation, asking for/giving advice/information, etc).
- When you write a transactional letter/email you should include **all** the relevant factual information given in the rubric, using your **own** words.
- You should also make sure that each paragraph deals with only one topic.

1 Read the advertisement and the two letters, then decide which model is good and which is bad, giving reasons for your answer.

MODEL A

Dear Sir/Madam,

I am writing to inquire about your advertisement in the September issue of Favourite Pets magazine. I am interested in dog obedience classes but I would be grateful if you could send me further details.

Firstly, I would like to know what breeds of dogs are accepted for the classes and whether the dog must be a certain age in order to take part. I have a six-month-old male cocker spaniel which I am anxious to train. He is very excitable and especially needs to learn how to walk without pulling on his lead.

I also require information on the cost of the course, when it will commence and how long it is likely to last.

I look forward to receiving details about the dog obedience classes. Thank you in advance for your help.

Yours faithfully,
Kristen Miller

MODEL B

Dear Sir/Madam,

I was reading the September issue of Favourite Pets magazine when I saw an ad for your dog-training school, so I decided to drop you a line. I need some information, you see.

My puppy is only six months old. Will you accept him at this age, or is he too young? He's really sweet. It would be great if you could let me know about this.

I'm sure that after taking your course my dog will be much easier to control, so I can't wait for it to start. When exactly do classes begin and end?

I'm looking forward to your reply. Thanks a lot.

Best wishes,
John Riley

Dog Obedience Classes

Train your dog in our special classes.
Register now for the autumn course.

For more information write to:
Smart Dogs
3, Longhill Green
Wolfhill

particular age or breed of dog?

when exactly do classes begin and end?

Notes:
- breed/age of dog
- specific aspects it needs training in
- cost of the course

Useful Language for Letters/Emails Requesting Information

Opening Remarks: (Formal) I am writing to inquire about/in connection with, etc.; (Informal) I want you to tell me; Can you let me know, etc. **To introduce first request**: (Formal) Could you possibly send; I would be grateful if you could; Would it be possible for you to tell/send me; I would appreciate some information about, etc. (Informal) Can you send/tell me, I want to know, etc.

To introduce further requests: (Formal) Could you also please send me; Another matter I need information on is; I would also like some information on, etc. (Informal) Can you also find out; I also want to know, etc.

Closing Remarks: (Formal) I look forward to receiving; I would appreciate it if you could inform me as soon as possible, etc. (Informal) Please, let me know; Send me the details; Tell me soon, etc.

2 **Read the instructions and the model email. Have all the points been covered in the email? What kind of email is it? Replace the underlined examples of useful language with similar ones from the table above.**

You belong to an activity club at school. At the last meeting, it was decided that the group would arrange a river-rafting trip. Your friends, Danny and Kim, went river-rafting last term with a school group, and you want to ask them about it.

Read the notes and then write an email to Danny and Kim, telling them about your plans and asking for information.

Dear Danny and Kim,

How are you both? Our school activity club is planning a river-rafting trip next month and I want you to tell me a few things since you went on a similar trip a little while ago.

Can you tell me how many students went on your trip? There are about thirty planning to go in our group. Do you think thatæs too many? Like you, we will probably just go for a day. Can you remember what the price was per person for a whole day of rafting?

I also want to know what it costs to hire a coach for one day. This would be helpful as that is how we intend to travel there.

Finally, did you have to take any special safety precautions to go rafting? Obviously we will want to be properly prepared and equipped before we start.

I hope you can help me with these details. Please let me know as soon as you can.

Love,
Sue

Notes:

- about 30 people
- one-day trip
- travel by coach

Questions to ask:

- How many were in your group?
- How much was coach hire?
- Price of full day of river-rafting per person?
- Any safety precautions taken?

Useful Expressions for Letters/Emails Giving Information

Opening Remarks: (Formal) I am writing in reply to your letter/email asking for information about/I am writing to inform you about; In reply to your query, etc. (Informal) This is what I found out ...; Remember the information you wanted?; You wanted me to tell you a few things about..., etc.
Closing Remarks: (Formal) I hope that I have been of some assistance to you; Please inform me if I can be of any further assistance/ I hope I have answered some of your questions; Please do not hesitate to contact me if you require any further information, etc. (Informal) I hope this will help you; Let me know if you need any more help..., etc.

3 **First read the advertisement (a) and the extract from Megan Jones' letter (b). Circle the key words in the extract which ask for information. Now, read Mr Williams' letter (c) and check if all the information is given. Finally, write down the topic of each paragraph.**

c

Dear Miss Jones,

I am writing in reply to your letter asking for information about our summer camp.

The camp lasts from July 22nd to August 30th. Our staff are required to work during the whole of this period. Regarding payment, we are offering a weekly wage of £70 plus free accommodation and food.

Accommodation includes a shared room with bathroom. There is a large on-site dining hall where campers and staff are provided with breakfast, lunch and dinner.

As far as the working day is concerned, we ask our leaders to be available for duty ten hours a day, including supervision time. Leaders are allowed one day off per week, but this is not to be taken at weekends.

I hope that I have been of some assistance to you. Please do not hesitate to contact me again if you require any further information.

Yours sincerely,
Gareth Williams

b

....
I would also like to know how long the summer camp lasts and what wages will be paid to the leaders. Could you also tell me what kind of accommodation is available and how many hours per day your leaders are required to work?
....
....

Yours sincerely,
Megan Jones

4 **Read the advertisement and the email of complaint. Then circle in the advertisement the points covered in the letter and make your own notes. The first one has been done for you as an example. How many complaints are stated and what reasons are given? Is it a mild or strong email of complaint? Justify your answer.**

Sunnysands Hotel

Come and stay at our glorious hotel, situated right on the sea front!

- tennis courts, swimming pool and gym facilities
- beautiful rooms with gorgeous sea views
- wonderful cuisine
- downstairs bar open until 2 am
- friendly staff

Our two-week package includes:

Transport to and from the airport, accommodation, buffet breakfast and three-course evening meal.

Write to:
Sunnysands Hotel@hotmail.com

closed for "cleaning" throughout our stay

New Message

Dear Sir/Madam,

I am writing to express my strong dissatisfaction with the holiday my wife and I had at your hotel in June.

Having paid for your all-inclusive package, we were upset, to say the least, when your coach did not come on time to take us to the hotel. However, to make matters worse, our room did not have a nice view at all. In fact, there was only a small window, which looked out onto filthy rubbish bins at the back of the hotel.

In addition, the food was tasteless and the service extremely slow. What is more, the noise from the bar kept us awake until 6am every morning, as the bar did not close at two, as stated in the advertisement. The last straw was when my wife went down for a swim on our second day, only to find that she could not swim as the pool was being cleaned. It remained closed for the rest of our holiday.

We feel that we should be fully compensated for our great disappointment with this holiday. We look forward to a reply at your earliest convenience.

Yours faithfully,
Alan Parker

5 **You attended an intensive Spanish course but you were dissatisfied with it. Using the advertisement and the notes you made, write a letter to complain about the course.**

Castile Spanish School Intensive Courses

Learn Spanish fast! Our system guarantees huge improvements in just two weeks.

- Accommodation with a Spanish family
- Intensive grammar course
- Debating to improve pronunciation and conversation skills
- Highly experienced tutors
- Trip to city museum

very unfriendly

mine wasn't!

cancelled & money not refunded

Style in Letters/Emails of Application

A letter/An email of application should be similar in style to the advertisement; that is, if the job advertisement is written in a less formal style, the letter/email could also be written in a less formal style. On the other hand, if the job advertisement is written in a formal style, the letter/email must be formal too.

Note: Advertisements for temporary jobs (holiday or summer jobs) may be written in a less formal style. A letter/An email of application for such a job may not include extensive reference to experience, qualifications or skills.

6 **Read the advertisement and the two letters which respond to it. Then answer the following questions: a) Is the advertisement formal or less formal? b) Which of the two letters uses the wrong style? Give reasons. c) What is the topic of each paragraph in MODEL B? Finally, underline expressions in both the advertisement and MODEL B which show the style of language that has been used.**

Questions to ask:

pay? *days off?*
hours? *meals?*

MODEL A

Dear Sir/Madam,

In response to your advertisement in this morning's *Brighton Advertiser* I would like to indicate my interest in the post of waiter.

I am twenty-two years old and have completed my B.A. in Oriental Studies. I plan to do a Master's degree in Medieval Chinese Literature in the next academic year, and am therefore seeking to improve my economic situation over the summer months.

I am highly qualified for a position of this kind. I am used to dealing with people as I am on the Executive Committee of the Student Union at City University. I would also like to ask about the following: the free days and the pay you offer. I trust meals are provided.

I look forward to hearing from you at your earliest convenience.

Yours faithfully,
James White

MODEL B

Dear Mr Murphy,

I saw your advertisement in the newspaper and I'm very interested in the waitressing job you are advertising.

I'm eighteen years old and I'm planning to go to university in September, so I'm looking for a job in order to earn some money.

I have done a lot of summer work in the past, including working in a coffee bar. I don't mind hard work and I learn quickly.

I've got a few questions, though, such as what pay you are offering and how many hours per day you will need me to work. Could you also tell me if I would get any days off and whether you provide any meals for your staff?

I'm looking forward to hearing from you soon.

Yours sincerely,
Celia Dobbs

7 **You have seen the job advertisement below. What notes would you make about the underlined words? Write an email of application for the post, including all the relevant information. Use an appropriate style.**

Busy high street music store requires part-time assistant to work <u>Saturdays</u> and <u>one evening per week</u>. <u>Pay</u> negotiable depending on experience.
Ideal job for someone interested in music.

Apply to: *Mr G. Jeffreys (Manager)*
RGMMusicStore@hotmail.com

8 **You are a former high school student trying to organise a reunion with classmates of ten years ago. Write a letter inviting them to the event. Using the notes and map below, include suitable information and directions from your old school to the Queen's Hotel in your letter.**

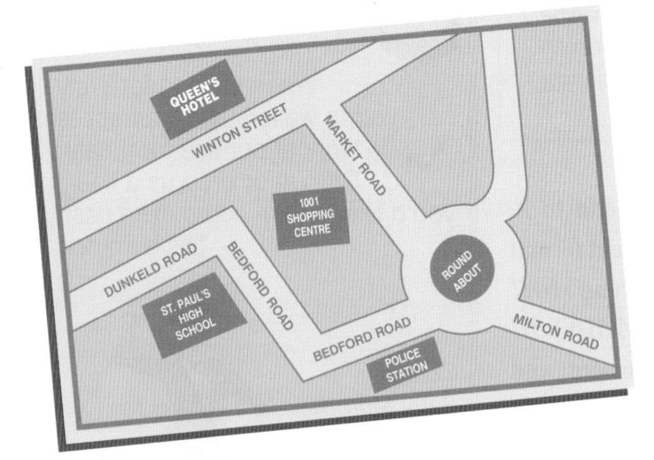

NOTES

Venue: Queen's Hotel
Date: Saturday 12th September
Time: 8.00 pm
Dress: formal

9 **Read the following topics. Then, say: a) what type and style of letter/email each one requires and b) which plan each letter/email should follow. How would you start and end each letter/email?**

1 You had an unpleasant experience while travelling abroad. Write a letter to a friend describing your experience and explaining why you will think twice before going abroad alone again.
2 Write an email to a friend telling him/her about a party you have recently been to, describing an interesting person that you met there.
3 You are in Paris and want to hire a car when you realise you have left your driving licence at home. Write a letter to your brother or sister asking for it to be sent to you by post. You should explain in your email where it can be found and why you need it.
4 You have to leave your present job due to family problems. Write a letter to your boss explaining why you have to leave the job, expressing regret and asking for a reference.
5 While your next-door neighbour is away on holiday, burglars broke into his/her house. Write an email to him/her saying what happened and giving advice on what he/she should do.
6 You and your friends have recently had a meal in an expensive restaurant. Write a letter to the manager of the restaurant expressing your satisfaction with the food but complaining about the service.
7 Write a letter to a member of your family inviting him/her to a family celebration, giving details of the event.
8 You have lost an important certificate which you need in order to apply for a job. Write a letter to the organisation from which the original certificate was issued, giving enough information about it so that you can be sent a copy.

Revision Box

10 **Mark the statements True or False justifying your answers.**

1 Letters/Emails are always formal in style. ☐
2 A letter/An email beginning "Dear Sir" must be signed "Yours faithfully". ☐
3 Letters/Emails of application should include information about qualifications and experience. ☐
4 The first paragraph of a letter/email usually states the reason for writing. ☐
5 Letters/Emails of complaint are always strong. ☐
6 A letter/An email of apology should not include explanations and reasons. ☐
7 A letter/An email beginning "Dear Mrs Perkins" is normally signed "Yours sincerely". ☐
8 Letters/Emails asking for advice should include reference to problems faced by the sender. ☐
9 Letters/Emails refusing an invitation need no reference to reasons why the sender cannot attend the event. ☐
10 Transactional letters/emails respond to advertisements only. ☐
11 Transactional letters/emails are always formal. ☐
12 The style of an application letter/email should correspond to the style of the job advertisement. ☐

Study Check 1

A Describe a festival you attended while on holiday in another country.

1 What kind of composition is this?
2 Which paragraph plan would you follow?
3 How would you begin your composition?
4 Which tenses would you use?
5 Which techniques would you use to make your description more vivid?
6 How would you end your description?

B Write a composition describing two people whom you often see.

1 What kind of composition is this?
2 Which paragraph plan would you follow?
3 Which tenses would you use?
4 Would you include narrative techniques in this composition?
5 How would you make your description more interesting?

C You have been asked to write a short story entitled "An Unforgettable Experience."

1 What should you decide on before starting to write your story?
2 Which tenses would you use throughout your story?
3 Which technique(s) would you choose to begin and end your story?
4 Which particular features would you include in order to make your story more interesting?

D You bought a portable CD player but after using it a couple of times it broke. Write a letter to the shop where you bought it asking to be given a replacement.

1 What kind of letter is this?
2 Which paragraph plan would you use?
3 Which opening and closing remarks would you use?
4 How would you support your complaints?
5 Which linking words could you use to join complaints with reasons?

E Write a letter to a new pen-friend who lives in another country. Describe yourself and give information about your hobbies, interests and ambitions.

1 What kind of letter is this?
2 Which paragraph plan would you use?
3 Which opening and closing remarks would you use?

F You have seen an advert for a holiday villa. Looking at the brochure and the notes you have made, write to the company asking for more information.

1 What kind of email is this?
2 Which paragraph plan should you follow?
3 What should you be careful to include when writing this type of email?
4 Which opening and closing remarks would you use?

UNIT 10 "For and Against" Essays

1 **Look at the pictures and think of as many advantages and disadvantages of living in the country as possible.**

2 **First read the table below, then listen to the cassette and tick the points mentioned. Which of these points are the advantages and which are the disadvantages of living in the country?**

A	no shops nearby	☐	E	safe place to bring up children	☐
B	no hospitals nearby	☐	F	far away from friends	☐
C	no noise from traffic	☐	G	long car journeys to school	☐
D	lower house prices	☐	H	healthy environment	☐

One type of argumentative essay is that which gives advantages and disadvantages (For and Against). It is a formal piece of writing in which a topic is considered from opposing points of view.

A good essay of this type should consist of:

a) **an introductory paragraph** in which you state the topic. This means that you talk generally about the topic without giving your opinion;

b) **a main body** in which the points for and the points against, along with your justification, appear in two separate paragraphs; and

c) **a closing paragraph** in which you give either your opinion or a balanced consideration of the topic.

Note: In this type of essay writing, you must **not** include opinion words (I believe, I think, etc.) in the introduction or the main body. Opinion words can **only** be used in the final paragraph, where you may state your opinion on the topic.

Points to consider

- Make a list of the points for and against a topic before you start writing.
- Write well-developed paragraphs in which the points you present are supported with justification, (i.e. reasons or examples). Make sure each paragraph has more than one sentence. *e.g. One advantage of using a word processor is that it saves time. It is much quicker to make corrections on one than it is to do them by hand.*
- Do not use informal style (e.g. short forms, colloquial language, etc.) or strong language (*e.g. I firmly believe,* etc.)
- Try to include a quotation relevant to the topic you are writing about. For example, if you are writing an essay on space exploration, a quotation you may include is: *"One small step for a man, one giant leap for mankind."* (Neil Armstrong)
- Begin each paragraph with a topic sentence which summarises what the paragraph is about.

topic sentence

However, there are disadvantages to owning a house.

point & justification

Firstly, it can be rather expensive and tiring to maintain. For example, repairs to the outside of the house can be costly, not to mention the time-consuming task of caring for a backyard or garden.

Introduction

Paragraph 1

state topic (summary of the topic without giving your opinion)

Main Body

Paragraph 2

arguments for *

Paragraph 3

arguments against *

Conclusion

Final Paragraph

balanced consideration/opinion

* *If you feel that there are more arguments for than against a topic, give them before the final paragraph to lead the reader to this conclusion.*

Linking Words/Phrases

To introduce points: one major advantage/disadvantage of, a further advantage, one point of view in favour of/against
To list points: in the first place, first of all, to start with, secondly, thirdly, finally, last but not least
To add more points to the same topic: what is more, furthermore, also, in addition to this/that, besides, apart from this/that, not to mention the fact that
To make contrasting points: on the other hand, however, in spite of, while, nevertheless, despite, even though, although, it can be argued that
To introduce examples: for example, for instance, like, especially, such as, in particular
To conclude: to sum up, all in all, all things considered, in conclusion, on the whole, taking everything into account, as was previously stated

3 Complete the following sentences, then replace the words in bold with other similar ones.

1 Public transport is often more convenient than taking one's car, **and is also** ....
2 Being able to speak a foreign language is very useful when abroad. **Furthermore,** ....
3 **Although** living abroad can be an interesting experience, ...
4 Being self-employed means that you are your own boss. **However,** ....
5 Exercise can help you to lose weight. **What is more,** ....
6 Experimenting on animals is cruel, **not to mention the fact that** ....
7 Package holidays are cheap. **On the other hand,** ....
8 **While** living alone can be lonely, it ....
9 Keeping up with fashion takes a lot of effort. **In addition,** ....
10 Watching television can be educational. **Nevertheless,** ....

You can end a "for and against" essay by a) giving a balanced consideration of the points on the topic or b) by giving your opinion, that is, for example, by expressing whether the advantages outweigh the disadvantages or vice versa.

4 Read the closing paragraphs below and say whether they express a balanced consideration or the writer's opinion.

1 In conclusion, getting married has, to my mind, more advantages than disadvantages. After all, what can be more fulfilling than a steady relationship with the person you love that lasts for the rest of your life?
2 To sum up, camping holidays do have advantages, the main one being that they are far cheaper than other holidays. In my opinion, however, there is too much hard work involved for them to ever feel like a real holiday.
3 To conclude, by looking after animals and helping them to breed, zoos play an important part in protecting many species from becoming extinct. Therefore, the negative aspects of keeping animals in captivity are balanced out by the positive ones.
4 All in all, computers have both advantages and disadvantages. They may have replaced humans in many jobs, but they have also made our lives considerably easier, and it is now difficult to imagine life without them.
5 On the whole, while most people go on holiday to rest, this is one thing you are unlikely to do on an adventure holiday. In my opinion, this disadvantage outweighs all the advantages associated with this kind of holiday.
6 Taking everything into account, there are both advantages and disadvantages in keeping pets. In the end it is up to the individual to decide whether the pleasure associated with owning a pet is worth the work that goes with it.

5 Give a one-minute talk on the topic of living in the country. Include linking words from the table above in your talk.

You can begin like this: Living in the country has always appealed to a lot of people. One advantage of ....

You can end like this: All things considered, ...
(Decide whether you want to give a balanced consideration or your opinion)

Techniques for beginnings and endings

The first paragraph may:

- make reference to a strange scene or situation, *e.g. Some scientists believe that in the future everyone will be genetically perfect.*
- address the reader directly, e.g. *Are you aware of any characteristics which you may have inherited from your parents?* or ask a rhetorical question (question to which no answer is expected), e.g. *Isn't it amazing how some children look so much like their parents?*
- start with a quotation, e.g. *"Genetics holds the key to the future"*

The last paragraph may:

- state a personal opinion, e.g. *In my opinion, I believe, In my view, It seems to me, The way I see it, I think, etc.*
- give the reader something to consider, e.g. *Perhaps the world would be a safer and more efficient place if everyone was genetically perfect.*
- end with a quotation, *e.g. "Genetics holds the key to the future"*, or a rhetorical question, *e.g. What will they think of next?*

6 Read the main body of the argumentative essay below on the topic *"Discuss the advantages and disadvantages of living in a foreign country"*. Then read the beginnings and endings and say which technique has been used in each one. Finally, replace the highlighted words or phrases in the main body with other synonymous words or phrases.

BEGINNINGS...

a Every morning some people strap on their skis, climb into their canoes or ride a horse to get to their jobs. They are not eccentrics, though; they have simply chosen to live in a place where ways of getting to work differ from those in their own country.

b As foreign travel becomes increasingly cheap and convenient, more and more people are discovering new places. Many prefer them to their own countries and decide to move there. But is living abroad as easy as it seems?

c Have you ever thought of settling down in your dream country? It is undoubtedly a big decision to make, but it can often change your life for the better.

One of the main advantages of living in a foreign country is that it gives you the opportunity to experience an entirely different way of life, which can be a valuable form of education. **Moreover**, one is given the chance to learn and become fluent in another language through everyday use. **In addition**, many people become more independent and self-reliant by having to cope with difficult situations on their own. **Finally**, living in a country with a different climate can prove beneficial to both one's health and state of mind.

On the other hand, even if you try your hardest to adapt to your new surroundings it is likely that you will often experience moments of isolation, frustration and loneliness. This can be caused by communication problems, especially if you cannot speak the language yet. **What is more**, finding a job can often be a stressful experience as in some countries foreigners are not easily accepted.

...ENDINGS

a To conclude, although living in a strange place can be stressful at first, it is something that almost everybody is capable of adjusting to. As Lydia Hearn once said, "A foreigner is only a foreigner until you've been introduced."

b In conclusion, living abroad is a good way to learn to co-exist with others. Perhaps if everyone experienced life in a foreign country, relations between countries might improve and the world would become a more peaceful place.

c However, in my view, living successfully in a foreign country depends on the individual. The more effort that is made to participate and become part of one's new surroundings, the more welcome and comfortable one will feel.

7 **Read the compositions and the table of "Do's" and "Don'ts". Find an example of each point in the models and write "Model A" or "Model B" next to it as well as the phrase/word itself, as in the example. Finally, decide which of the two compositions is a good model, give the paragraph plan and say what a successful argumentative essay (for and against) should or should not contain.**

MODEL A

"Discuss the advantages and disadvantages of being your own boss."

Have you ever considered becoming your own boss? In recent years the number of people choosing to start their own business has risen significantly. Many claim that this is because more and more people are no longer content to work for someone else.

One of the main advantages of being self-employed is the fact that you are completely self-reliant and can make decisions on your own. This can give you a great sense of freedom and allows you to do exactly what you want without interference from anyone else. What is more, your working day can be planned for your convenience, allowing you to work when you want rather than when you have to. Finally, if your business is successful, people will know that you alone should be given the credit.

However, there are disadvantages to being your own boss. Many self-employed people have said that to build a successful business, you have to be prepared to work long hours and sacrifice your personal life. As B. C. Forbes once said, "If you don't drive your business, you will be driven out of business." Moreover, a 1996 government study found that over a quarter of the businesses run by newly self-employed people failed within the first two years.

All things considered, it seems to me that self-employment can be a very gratifying experience, although not one without difficulties. But when success is achieved, the greatest reward of all is the knowledge that you have done it on your own.

MODEL B

"Discuss the advantages and disadvantages of being your own boss."

In my opinion, self-employment has various advantages, though there are some bad points too.

Working for yourself can be a positive experience. Everybody wants to have their own business and even my uncle has opened his own shop. Statistics show that more and more people are quitting their jobs and starting their own business. I think that the best thing about it is that you can do what you want and nobody can tell you off. But then again, you usually have to work really hard if you're on your own and everyone knows that it's a big responsibility to run your own business.

You can choose how much you want to work and you can stop if you feel like it, when you're your own boss. The only bad thing is that you may have to spend your own money to make the business work. Everyone wants to have their own business and for some people it works well. This is a good reason for them to feel proud because they've done it all by themselves.

Having your own business can be very difficult but for some people it's worth it because they don't mind the hard work and they end up making a lot of money and feel good about themselves.

DO's

- formal style - Model A, *e.g. the .. number of ... has risen significantly*
- well-developed paragraphs - .....
  ....
- justification of arguments - ....
  ....
- linking words/phrases - ....
  ....
- quotations - ....
  ....
- generalisations - ....
  ....
- reference to specific statistics -
  ....
- opinion only in the last paragraph - ....

DON'Ts

- informal style (short forms) - .....
  ....
- one sentence paragraphs - ....
  ....
- overgeneralisations - ....
  ....
- personal examples - ....
  ....
- opinion in the first paragraph -
  ....
- blind use of statistics - ....
  ....

8 **Read through the arguments and match each argument with its corresponding justification. Then say which are in favour of and which are against using mobile phones.**

Arguments	Justification
1 Using mobile phones can be dangerous.	a If you find yourself in a dangerous situation, you can call for help no matter where you are.
2 Mobile phones are very useful for people who are often on the move.	b Talking on a mobile phone while driving reduces concentration by up to 30% and so greatly increases the chances of causing an accident.
3 Some people claim that owning a mobile phone is a waste of money.	c They can easily be contacted no matter where they are.
4 Having a mobile phone increases your personal security.	d The basic charge for the service is much higher than for a normal telephone, and the calls are extremely expensive.

9 **Read the quotations and the paragraphs below, then decide which quotation should be included in each paragraph and write it in the space provided.**

Quotations

a "Without the past the pursued future has no meaning."
b "Advertising is the art of making whole lies out of half truths."
c "Prisons as they are do not teach a person to live in society – they teach him to live in prison."
d "The scientists split the atom; now the atom is splitting us."

1 One thing that counts against advertising is the fact that it plays a far larger role than it should in society today and often deliberately misinforms the public about the product being promoted. As Edgar A. Shoaff said, ...
2 Although technology has made our lives easier in many ways, it has also created new problems for mankind. As Quentin Reynolds said, ... But while it has created problems, we should think carefully before dismissing its many benefits.
3 It has been said by Loren Eiseley, an American anthropologist, that ...., and in today's world this is truer than ever. All too often, history seems to repeat itself, something that could be avoided if we were to pay more attention to the past.
4 To conclude, it is clear that a long-term solution to the problem is to discourage young people from becoming criminals rather than to punish them afterwards. As Alan Bartholemew once said, ...

10 **Match the quotations with the composition topics.**

Quotations

1 "It is only when they go wrong that machines remind you how powerful they are." (Clive James)
2 "A man travels the world in search of what he needs and returns home to find it." (George Moore)
3 "All men are creative, but few are artists." (Paul Goodman)
4 "The car has become an article of dress without which we feel uncertain, unclad and incomplete." (Marshall McLuhan)

Topics

a What are the advantages and disadvantages of owning a car?
b "Travelling has both advantages and disadvantages." Discuss.
c What are the advantages and disadvantages of the increasing use of technology?
d Discuss the advantages and disadvantages of being a professional artist.

11 **Write these essays in the appropriate style using 120 - 180 words.**

1 Your teacher has asked you to write a composition giving arguments for and against owning a mobile phone.
2 You have been asked to write a composition on the advantages and disadvantages of living in the country.

12 **Read the essay below and state the topic of each paragraph. How does it begin and end? Fill in the correct linking word or phrase. Finally, list the advantages and disadvantages mentioned.**

"The advantages and disadvantages of owning a pet."

Many types of animals have gradually become domesticated and have been taken into our homes as pets. Pets are enjoyed by young and old alike, but are they really worth having or are there too many drawbacks?

1) ...., pets can be great companions for those who live alone, such as the elderly. What is more, having a dog around the house can give you a greater sense of security. 2) ...., young children usually love animals and giving them the opportunity to look after a pet teaches them to care for living things and to be responsible.

3) ...., bringing a pet into your home is not a decision to be taken lightly. There are some expenses involved as animals need food, special cages, equipment and occasional veterinary treatment which can be costly. They 4) .... need care and attention on a daily basis, which can be time-consuming. 5) ...., a pet ties you down to a certain extent. You cannot just get up and go away for the weekend or for a holiday without first taking your pet´s needs into consideration. This is not always easy and can be expensive if you have to pay for professional care.

6) ...., buying a pet should be a carefully planned decision. If you are fully aware of your pet´s needs and all the responsibilities involved in owning one, then having a pet can be a very rewarding experience.

3

The block of flats where I live is close to the city centre. It's very convenient for me.

13 **Read what the people in the pictures say about living in a block of flats. Who speaks in favour of it and who is against? Can you think of any other advantages and disadvantages? Finally, write a composition of 120 - 180 words on this topic. Use linking words/phrases.**

14 ***"The advantages and disadvantages of watching TV."***

Think of as many points for and against watching TV as possible. Then, write an essay on this topic using 120 - 180 words. Remember to use appropriate linking words or phrases.

15 **Put these jumbled sentences in the correct order. Then write them out in two separate paragraphs, one including all the advantages, the other all the disadvantages. Finally, write a suitable beginning and ending for this topic.**

Package holidays: Good or Bad?

☐ **A** However, there are disadvantages to going on a package holiday.

☐ **B** To start with, package holidays are cheaper than travelling on your own, as the price includes the air fare and hotel accommodation.

☐ **C** Another negative aspect is that as you have paid for your accommodation in advance, you often feel obliged to stay in that place rather than move around and explore.

☐ **D** Furthermore, the brochures from which most people select a package holiday usually give you a good idea of what the resort offers, therefore reducing the chances of disappointment.

☐ **E** Package holidays have several advantages.

☐ **F** In the first place, as package holidays are less expensive, the hotel is unlikely to be top-class.

☐ **G** Last but not least, when visiting a new place it is often much easier to have all the details arranged in advance as it can be rather confusing to plan everything by yourself.

☐ **H** Also package holiday destinations are usually popular tourist resorts, thus there is little opportunity to experience the true culture of the country you are visiting.

16 **Rewrite the following text by linking the sentences in each paragraph. Use appropriate linking words or phrases.**

"The advantages and disadvantages of being famous."

People who are famous are usually financially secure. They are often given free designer clothes, cars and jewellery by manufacturers who receive free advertising when these items are worn or used. They receive first-class service wherever they go. They have the power to influence other people and are even role models to many. They have domestic help and employ staff to take care of their business. They are confident and secure as they are successful professionals.

They seldom have privacy and often have to go out in public wearing a disguise so that they will not be recognised. Many people take advantage of them and they often lead lonely lives as they never know who their real friends are. Many end up having nervous breakdowns because of stress. Some live in fear of being or having members of their family kidnapped. People expect them to look glamorous and happy at all times, which is hard for celebrities to do.

17 *"The advantages and disadvantages of going to work by car."*

First, think of as many points for and against going to work by car as possible. Then, listen to the cassette to find out whether you have thought of the same points. You may take notes while listening. Finally, write an essay on this topic using 120 - 180 words.
Remember to use appropriate linking words or phrases.

UNIT 11 Opinion Essays

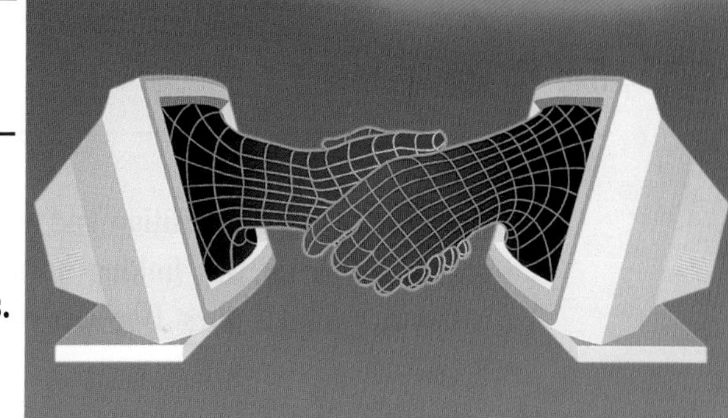

1 **Discuss the good and bad points of using the Internet.**

2 **Listen to the cassette and match the viewpoints with the reasons. Who speaks in favour of using the Internet and who speaks against it?**

	Viewpoints	Reasons
Paul	A great way of communicating with people from all over the world	1 saves time going to libraries; is fast and cheap to send messages
Julie	B people should be more careful about how they use it	2 have conversations with people from different places
Joe	C great way of getting information quickly	3 some of the information you can access is not suitable, especially for children

- Opinion essays are formal in style. They require your opinion on a topic which must be clearly stated and supported by reasons. It is necessary to include the opposing viewpoint in another paragraph.

  A successful opinion essay should have:
  a) an **introductory paragraph** in which you state the topic and your opinion;
  b) a **main body** which consists of two or more paragraphs. Each paragraph should present a separate viewpoint supported by your reasons. Another paragraph giving the opposing viewpoint and reasons may be included; and
  c) a **conclusion** in which you restate your opinion using different words.

Points to consider

- First decide whether you agree or disagree with the subject of the topic and make a list of your points and reasons.
- Write well-developed paragraphs consisting of more than one sentence.
- Begin each paragraph with a topic sentence which summarises what the paragraph is about.
- Linking words should be used throughout your composition.
- Use the techniques shown on p. 66 to begin and end your essay.

Useful Language

To express opinion: I believe, In my opinion, I think, In my view, I strongly believe, The way I see it, It seems to me (that)
To list points: In the first place, first of all, to start with, Firstly, to begin with
To add more points: what is more, another major reason, also, furthermore, moreover, in addition to this/that, besides, apart from this, not to mention the fact that
To introduce contrasting viewpoints: It is argued that, People argue that, Opponents of this view say, There are people who oppose, Contrary to what most people believe, As opposed to the above ideas
To introduce examples: for example, for instance, such as, in particular, especially
To conclude: To sum up, All in all, All things considered, Taking everything into account

Introduction

Paragraph 1

state the topic and your opinion clearly

Main Body

Paragraph 2

viewpoint 1 and reason

Paragraph 3 *

viewpoint 2 and reason

Paragraph 4

give the opposing viewpoint and reasons

Conclusion

Final Paragraph

restate your opinion, using different words

* *you may include more viewpoints, and therefore more paragraphs in the main body*

3 **Read the model composition and write down the topic of each paragraph. Underline any linking words or phrases and replace them with other similar ones. How else could you start this essay?**

state the topic (summary of the topic and your opinion)

"Are you in favour of or against exams being abolished?"

Is too much emphasis placed on examination results today? In my view, their role needs to be re-examined if they are to continue to play a part in the educational system.

In the first place, exams do not actually test a person's knowledge of a subject but rather how much they can remember on the day of the exam. In addition, facts such as students feeling unwell or suffering from a case of nerves on the day of the exams are not taken into consideration.

Furthermore, the exam system is unfair to people who have studied hard but have a poor memory for facts and figures. Also, it is often the case that people who have not studied can copy from someone else who has.

It is argued that exams are the most efficient way of comparing the abilities of a group of people and that an exam will often encourage people to compete to get better grades. Making grades and exam results the main point of learning though, gives students the wrong idea of what education is all about.

In conclusion, it seems to me unfair to give a person only one chance to show what they are capable of. I think that the whole educational system needs to be changed so that exams are not the only way of assessing a student's knowledge.

4 ***"Cars are the greatest danger to human life today."*** **Give your opinion with reasons. Then read what these people think about cars and match their viewpoints with their reasons. Suggest various ways to begin and end this opinion essay as shown on p. 66. Finally, write a composition on this topic.**

1

2

3

4

a It is people themselves who cause the greatest harm to society, not technology or machines as such. Cars are not at all dangerous if they're driven with care and attention.

b Every day we hear about fatal car accidents. Increasingly often people are killed or seriously injured on the roads.

c Exhaust fumes are one of the major causes of air pollution and as a result, our health is at risk as well as the environment.

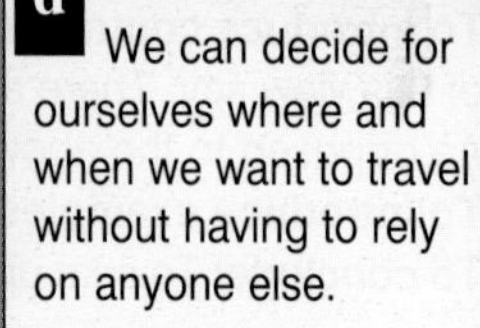

d We can decide for ourselves where and when we want to travel without having to rely on anyone else.

5 First give your opinions and reasons concerning the topic below, then read the model and give the topic of each paragraph. Next, replace the highlighted linking words with similar ones. Finally, underline the reason given for each viewpoint. Which quotation is included in this essay? Which techniques have been used to begin and end the essay?

People spend too much time and money on fashion.
Do you agree or disagree?

Every season, the great fashion houses of Europe and America present their new collections in the hope of persuading people to renew their wardrobes by purchasing the latest designs. In my opinion, one does not have to be a slave to fashion in order to look smart.

To start with, following the latest trends in fashion can be extremely expensive. This is especially true for those who buy costly designer clothing. There is also the risk of getting into debt in order to keep up with the latest fashions.

In addition to this, followers of fashion often give up their individuality for the sake of fashion. They choose clothes which suit neither their figures nor their personalities. This is unfortunate, as the way we dress should reflect who we really are.

On the other hand, some people argue that it is necessary to dress fashionably in order to create the correct image for their careers. This is particularly true of those who work with the public, as they reflect the image of their company. This does not mean that the latest fashions are the most appropriate, however. Simple but well-made clothes are almost always the best choice for business wear.

To conclude, I strongly believe that it is advisable to dress with style by choosing good quality clothes which suit you as an individual and have lasting elegance. As the famous designer Coco Chanel put it, "Fashion is made to become unfashionable." So instead of changing your wardrobe constantly, isn't it better to build up a collection of clothes which you can always wear?

6 Read the essay on the topic: ***Will life be better in the future?*** and answer these questions: Which paragraph(s) a) state the writer's opinion? b) give the other side of the argument? What tenses are used and why? Which are the topic sentences?

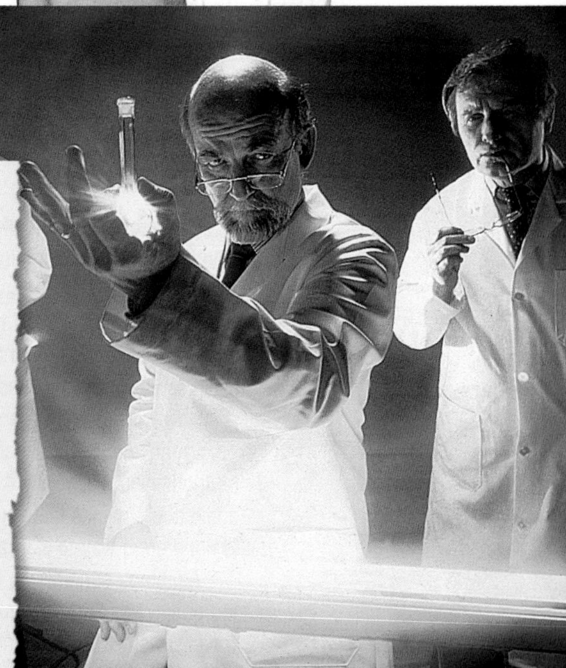

Can you imagine doing your shopping without having to leave the house, or working at home rather than going to the office? In my opinion, life in the future will be much more pleasant than it is today.

In the first place, there will be many improvements in the field of medicine. Scientists are confident that cures for diseases such as cancer and AIDS will have been found. Therefore, the lives of thousands of people will be saved.

Also, new technological breakthroughs will make our lives easier. Computers will be able to perform more time-saving functions, transport will be faster and more efficient and new inventions will continue to help us carry out daily tasks with ease and comfort.

On the other hand, there are those who believe that life in the the future will not be so trouble-free. We will have used up the world's natural resources, therefore our planet will be on the verge of destruction. What is more, some fear that pollution will have increased due to problems such as deforestation, and that acid rain will only have been made worse. They do not consider, however, that modern technology can solve environmental problems as well as less pressing ones.

All in all, I feel that life in the future will definitely be better. We are all searching for ways to improve our lives and we can only look ahead in order to do this.

7 **Read the following models and answer these questions: a) Which is a "for and against" argumentative essay? b) Which are the "for and against" points mentioned? c) Which is an opinion essay? d) How is each viewpoint supported? Finally, write down the topic of each paragraph. In what ways do these models differ?**

"The aeroplane is the most convenient means of travel." Give your opinion on this statement.

MODEL A

Over the past few years, people have begun to travel to places they would only have dreamt of visiting thirty years ago, thanks to the possibilities offered by air travel. In my opinion, travelling by aeroplane cannot be compared with any other means of transport.

To start with, there really is no faster way to travel. You can go from one country to another in a matter of hours which gives you more time to enjoy the actual purpose of your trip, rather than waste time travelling and dragging your luggage around.

Furthermore, you always feel well looked after on an aeroplane. You are served drinks and meals and offered newspapers and blankets which all help to make the journey more comfortable and enjoyable.

Of course, there are people who argue that travelling by plane can be a nightmare, with airport delays, cramped seats and turbulence to put up with. What is more, aeroplanes and airports are often targeted by terrorists, which makes some people think that travelling by plane is unsafe. They forget, however, that the number of deaths caused by cars is larger than that caused by planes.

In my opinion, air travel will always remain popular. Its speed, comfort and convenience are hard to beat.

8 **The techniques used to begin and end a "for and against" argumentative essay can also be used to begin and end an opinion essay. Remember that in a "for and against" essay your opinion is mentioned in the last paragraph only, whereas in an opinion essay your opinion should be mentioned in both the first and last paragraphs. Refer to the theory box on page 66, then write different beginnings and endings for Models A and B practising the techniques mentioned.**

"Discuss the advantages and disadvantages of travelling by plane."

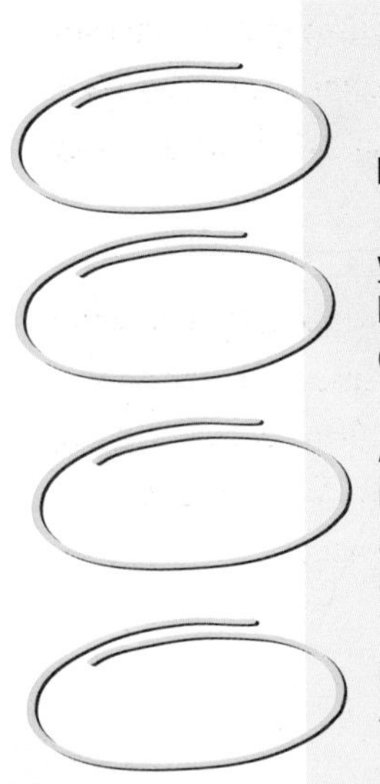

MODEL B

The aeroplane is one of the most popular and widely used forms of transport today. However, it does have both its advantages and disadvantages, as outlined below.

To begin with, you always feel that you are well looked after when travelling by plane. Once you have checked your luggage in, you need not worry about it until you reach your destination. What is more, once you are on board the plane, you are made to feel comfortable and are served refreshments and meals by friendly, helpful cabin crew. Finally, the speed of an aircraft ensures that you will reach your destination in a matter of hours.

However, air travel can be expensive and there are often long delays in airports which can be irritating. Also, many people are afraid of flying, and the cramped seats and claustrophobic atmosphere of a plane can be frightening, especially if there is turbulence. What is more, travelling from one time zone to another within a few hours means that you are likely to suffer from jet lag. This can take up to a week to recover from, which is not a good way to start a holiday.

All things considered, it seems that although air travel does have its bad points, it has one overwhelming positive aspect — the fact that it is far quicker than any other means of transport. This means that most travellers are willing to ignore its drawbacks if it means that they are able to make their journeys shorter.

9 Match the viewpoints with the reasons in the boxes. Then write an essay of 120 – 180 words on the topic: *Has genetic science gone too far?*

Reasons

A ☐ Once scientists have perfected the technique of cloning prime sheep and cows for food, there will be plenty to eat for everyone.

B ☐ We are working against nature, which is dangerous, and we have no idea what effect it will have on the natural order of things.

C ☐ Scientists should stop and consider whether their experiments will benefit mankind or not before it is too late.

D ☐ Imagine if scientists find a way to create human beings in a completely artificial way.

E ☐ It can help to trace diseases and may help to save the lives of millions of people around the world. Eventually, we may be able to eliminate all terminal illnesses.

10 Give your viewpoints with reasons on the topic: *Was life better in the past?* Now listen to the cassette and check which of your viewpoints have been mentioned. Are there any viewpoints you had not thought of?

11 Read the following topics and say a) which is a "for and against" essay and which is an opinion essay, b) what plan should be followed for each topic? Then suggest possible beginnings and endings for each topic.

1 Your teacher has asked you to write a composition on the topic: *Cinema will soon be a thing of the past*. Write a composition for your teacher.

2 Your school newspaper needs an article about the *advantages and disadvantages of being a professional sportsman.* Write an article for the newspaper.

3 Your local newspaper is investigating the question: *Are newspapers necessary nowadays?* Write an essay on the topic.

4 Your teacher has asked you to write a composition discussing *the advantages and disadvantages of keeping animals in zoos.* Write a composition for your teacher.

UNIT 12 Providing Solutions to Problems Essays

1 Look at the table below, then listen to the cassette and match the suggestions with the results. What is the subject of the meeting?

Suggestions	Results
1 daily rubbish collection	a reduce amount of rubbish to be collected and save natural resources
2 better recycling system	b live in healthier surroundings
3 fine people who drop litter	c prevent the spread of diseases
4 tyre factory to shut down	d less litter on the streets

An essay in which we suggest solutions to a problem is a formal piece of writing. For each suggestion made, we should mention any expected results or consequences.

A good essay providing solutions to problems should consist of:

a) an **introductory paragraph** which states the problem (reasons why it has arisen can also be included);

b) a **main body** in which we present our suggestions and results/consequences (remember to begin a new paragraph for each suggestion made); and

c) a **closing paragraph** in which we summarise our opinion.

Useful Language

To introduce suggestions: To begin/start with, One way to, Another solution would be ..., Another way to ... would be ...

To express cause: because of/owing to/due to the fact that, for this reason

To express effect: thus, therefore, as a result, consequently, so, as a consequence

To express reality: in fact, as a matter of fact, actually, in practice

To emphasise what you say: obviously, clearly, needless to say, in particular

To conclude: All in all, To sum up, All things considered

Introduction

Paragraph 1

state the problem

Main Body

Paragraph 2

suggestion 1 & result

Paragraph 3 *

suggestion 2 & result

Conclusion

Final Paragraph

summarise opinion

* *The main body can consist of more than two paragraphs depending on the number of suggestions you want to make.*

2 Read the following essay and give the topic of each paragraph. Then replace the underlined words/phrases with other similar ones.

"What can we do to reduce global litter?"

Global litter is an ongoing concern which many nations have to deal with. Fortunately, there are a number of possible solutions which could lead to a permanent reduction in the waste that has mounted up in countries around the world.

One way would be to encourage companies to use bio-degradable packaging for their products. Bio-degradable items decompose naturally and therefore they do not add to the problem of litter.

Another solution would be to save scrap metal in order to put it to further use. As a result, all discarded metal products such as vehicles, water tanks and machine parts could be melted down and used to make other products.

The most effective method of reducing litter, however, is to educate people to recycle their household waste products. In fact, schemes such as paper saving, bottle banks and aluminium can collections have all been successful in reducing litter in many countries.

All things considered, there are many solutions to the problem of global litter. The sooner these solutions are put into action, the more significant the reduction in global litter will be.

3 Match each suggestion with the corresponding result and link them with an appropriate word/phrase from the list below.

thus, therefore, so, as a result, consequently

Suggestions

1 One way to solve famine disasters in third-world countries is for the rest of the world to provide them with the financial aid they need in order to build extensive irrigation systems.
2 One way to help reduce pollution in large cities would be to encourage people to only drive vehicles which run on lead-free fuel.
3 It has been suggested that one way of helping homeless people is for authorities to accommodate them in low-cost hostels.
4 Another solution would be for the social services to pay unemployment benefit for a limited time only.
5 One way for people to use up excess energy is to take up a sport of some kind.

Results

a They would have a secure base from which to rebuild their lives and perhaps find jobs.
b They would be more relaxed and suffer less stress.
c They would be able to grow their own crops successfully and increase their food supplies.
d There would be less air pollution due to the reduction in harmful exhaust fumes.
e More people would be encouraged to enter the workforce as soon as possible.

4 You belong to an environmental group. Read the following suggestions, then write an article in 120-180 words to be used in the magazine your group is planning to publish. Your article will be entitled:*"How we can save the environment."*

5 **A weekly newspaper has asked its readers to suggest ways to improve the kind of help we give to famine victims. Read the following letter and fill in the appropriate linking words, then say which suggestions have been put forward and what the results/consequences of each suggestion would be.**

another solution would be, all in all, due to the fact that, another way, furthermore, to begin with, thus, in this way, as a result

Dear Sir,

I feel that the aid we give to famine victims at the moment is simply not sufficient. This is partly **1)** ...*due to the fact that*... there is not enough money available for famine relief, and current supplies of food and medicine are being wasted or stolen. Famine victims need permanent solutions as well as immediate help.

2) ...., much more money could be raised by holding charity concerts and other money-raising events. **3)** ...., international organisations would receive the money they need to provide emergency famine relief and **4)** .... be able to save thousands of lives.

5) .... of helping victims would be for wealthy countries to send food and medical supplies directly to areas affected by famine. **6)** ...., by improving administration and transport, supplies would be certain to reach those people who really need them.

7) .... to educate farmers in famine areas so that they could improve their farming techniques, **8)** .... making sure that famine is less likely to occur in the future.

9) ...., it is extremely difficult to solve the problem of famine. If, however, the matter is taken seriously and world leaders join together to find solutions, the situation can be improved.

Yours faithfully,
Thomas Wilson

6 **Read the following essay and fill in the gaps with the appropriate topic sentences.**

A *An additional technique is to use the movement of the ocean tides to generate power.*
B *One alternative which is already widely used is nuclear power.*
C *All things considered, the need to develop alternative energy sources is of vital importance.*
D *Another alternative source of energy is solar power.*

Coal will not last forever. What alternative sources of energy can we use?

Coal is a "non-renewable" resource. This means that once it has been used up, it is gone forever. The use of coal is also environmentally harmful. Consequently, the development of alternative sources of energy is very important.

[1] A single power station of this type can satisfy the energy needs of a whole city and does not pollute the air. Therefore, air quality is improved in countries which use this technology. However, it does produce radioactive waste which is difficult to dispose of.

[2] It is a very low-cost source of energy, therefore more and more countries have started using the sun's energy to produce electricity.

[3] Incoming and outgoing tides can turn huge pieces of machinery to create electricity. As a result, the forces of nature are used to provide a clean, renewable source of energy.

[4] There are some promising techniques already in use, but more research needs to be done before we can stop being dependent on fossil fuels.

7 **Your teacher has asked you to write a composition entitled:** ***Discuss ways to improve the learning of foreign languages.*** **Read the suggestions made by some students. What results do you think these would have? Now write a composition of 120-180 words on the topic.**

We could watch more films in the language we are trying to learn.

We should listen to and sing songs in the language.

It would be a good idea to participate in student exchange programmes or to organise trips abroad.

We should make more use of newspapers, magazines and other authentic reading material such as brochures and leaflets.

UNIT 13 Discursive Essays

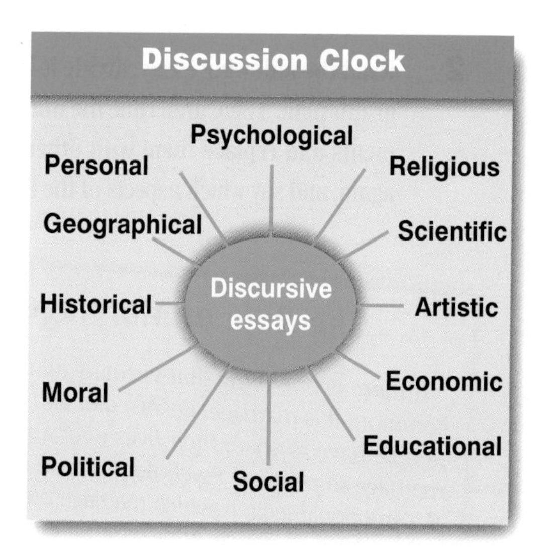

1 **Look at the discussion clock, then listen to two people talking about sport and whether it is valuable to our society. Say which aspects from the discussion clock are discussed.**

Discursive essays are formal in style. In this type of essay, the writer focuses on various aspects of the topic in turn. Some possible aspects to be considered are set out in the "discussion clock" on this page (moral, political, social, etc.). Each viewpoint is supported by examples. Opposing viewpoints should be mentioned as well. These essays do not aim to persuade the reader that the writer's opinion is the only valid one, but to make him/her consider a current issue from various angles, allowing him/her to form his/her own opinion or expand on the viewpoints already mentioned. A good discursive essay should consist of:

a) an **introduction** in which you state the topic, explaining the current or past situation;

b) a **main body** consisting of two or more paragraphs, in each of which a viewpoint is discussed along with the opposing viewpoint; and

c) a **conclusion** in which you summarise the topic by making a general comment about it. Your opinion can also be included.

Points to consider

- When considering a topic, bear in mind the "discussion clock". This will help you decide on what viewpoints to mention in the essay. Each topic can be seen from various viewpoints.
- Before writing your discursive essay, decide on the viewpoints you will mention. Keep in mind that you cannot approach a topic through *all* the aspects presented in the discussion clock. The various aspects illustrated are there to help you plan your essay.
- Remember that for each viewpoint you have thought of, there is an opposing argument. Think of the opposing arguments while planning your essay.
- Join the opposing viewpoints with appropriate linking words such as **however, on the other hand, on the contrary,** and **contrary to.**
- Avoid using simplistic words. Instead, use more sophisticated vocabulary.

Useful Language for Discursive Essays

To bring up other points or aspects: as far as, regarding, as for, with regard to
To make contrasting points: yet, however, nevertheless, although, in spite of, despite, while, on the other hand, it is argued that, opponents of this view say, there are people who oppose, contrary to what people believe
To conclude: all in all, to sum up, in my opinion, in my view, to my mind
To express reality: in fact, as a matter of fact, in practice, the fact is

Introduction

state the topic

Main Body

Paragraph 2

first viewpoint & opposing argument

Paragraph 3 *

second viewpoint & opposing argument

Conclusion

summarise topic, making general comments, and/or giving your opinion

* *The main body can consist of more than two paragraphs depending on the number of viewpoints you want to talk about*

2 Read the following essay, divide it into paragraphs and give the paragraph plan. Then, underline the words used to introduce opposing arguments and replace them with other synonymous ones. Finally, read it again, and say which aspects of the discussion clock have been covered.

The Role of Marriage in Today's Society

If there is one thing that virtually all the world's various cultures have in common, it is marriage. Beliefs, diet and languages vary greatly, but the desire people have to share their lives with another seems universal. Why then, is marriage so popular? Psychologists have said that people have a deep need for the emotional security which marriage provides. Knowing that one has a partner in life makes it easier to cope with the problems of daily life. On the other hand, the fact that many single people are content to live alone suggests that the "emotional need" theory is incomplete. British novelist Fay Weldon once stated, "Marriage has nothing to do with emotion and everything to do with property." According to the supporters of this view, people marry in order to increase their wealth, either by marrying a rich partner or because, as the saying goes, "two can live as cheaply as one." It is true that financial considerations are often the primary reason that people marry. Yet there are countless examples of people "marrying for love", regardless of their mate's lack of money. All in all, marriage continues to be extremely popular in many societies. Most of us have a need for love and support and want to have children at some point in our lives. Fully understanding the reasons why people marry, though, may be as difficult as understanding the human mind itself.

3 Match each viewpoint with its opposing argument. Can you suggest other opposing arguments? Replace the underlined words with other synonymous ones.

Viewpoints

1 From an educational standpoint, it is vital that historical sites be preserved, so that we can teach our children about their cultural heritage.

2 From a social viewpoint, voluntary services play an important role. They help people in remote areas or poverty-stricken regions by offering medical assistance and even providing food in some cases.

3 From a moral point of view, censorship protects people from being exposed to material that may disturb or offend them, such as violent scenes in films.

4 From a scientific standpoint, the development of nuclear technology has led to significant advances. For example, nuclear energy is a clean way of providing power to our cities.

Opposing Arguments

a **Nevertheless**, it can be argued that everyone has a different idea of what is moral and acceptable and what is not. Certainly, what offends one person may not offend another.

b **On the other hand**, some educators argue that the money used for preserving sites should go to improving the educational system. In this way, children will benefit more.

c **Opponents argue** that nuclear technology has produced deadly bombs and has forced people to live in fear.

d **However**, one problem with these groups is that in order to exist, they depend entirely on donations from private individuals.

4 **Replace the words in bold with synonymous words or phrases.**

1 **As far as** education **is concerned**, computers may now have as much to offer as books.
2 **However**, children brought up by parents of different nationalities tend to be bilingual from a very early age.
3 **I personally believe that** if everyone made a little more effort, we could successfully save our environment from further destruction.
4 It is often argued that prison sentences discourage crime, but **in practice** imprisonment seems to have little effect on the crime rate.
5 **With regard to** the health benefits of vegetarianism, there are strong arguments for both sides of the subject.
6 **Nevertheless**, it cannot be denied that there are far more similarities than differences between the abilities of boys and girls.
7 **In my view**, children who live in cities should all be given the opportunity to experience the pleasures of the countryside.
8 **In fact,** declining educational standards suggest that television is harmful to learning, rather than a useful learning tool.

5 **Look at the following diagram. What aspects of the discussion clock have been covered? Now, read the opposing arguments and match them with the viewpoints mentioned in the diagram. Then, write your essay on the topic: *The usefulness of computers.***

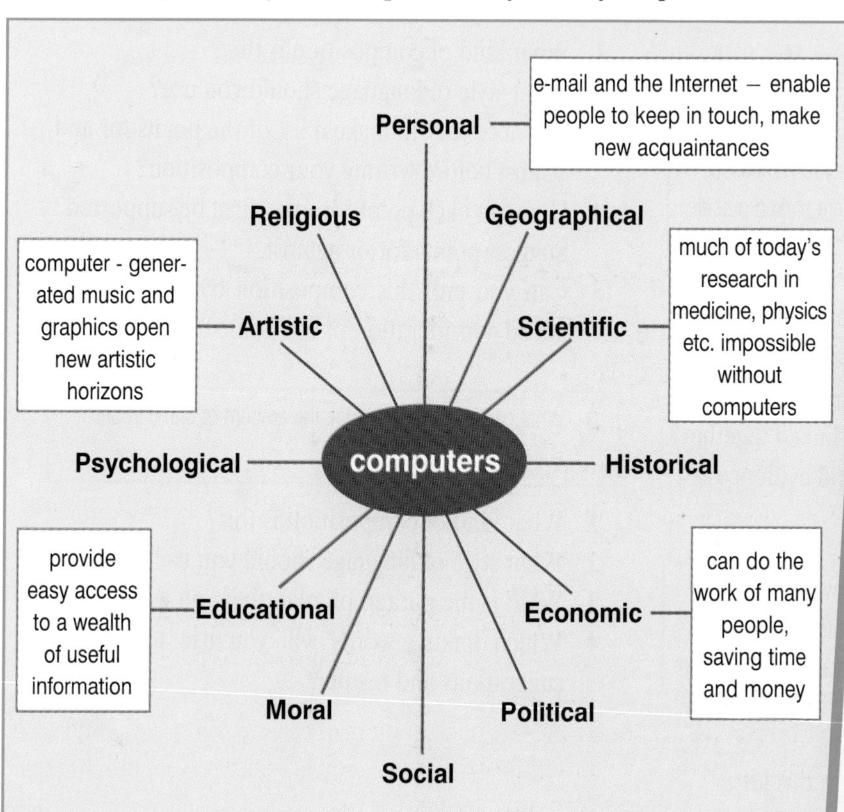

Revision Box

6 **Mark the statements True or False justifying your answers.**

1 Each paragraph should begin with a topic sentence. ☐
2 Statistics can be referred to even if you are not certain of the source. ☐
3 When providing solutions to problems you should not mention the results of the solutions suggested. ☐
4 A discursive essay should be formal. ☐
5 Linking words should be used in all kinds of argumentative compositions. ☐
6 In the conclusion of a "for and against" essay you should give either a balanced consideration of the topic or your own opinion. ☐
7 An informal style is always used when writing argumentative compositions. ☐
8 In a discursive essay you may discuss one viewpoint and its opposing argument in the same paragraph. ☐

Opposing arguments:

1 keep young people from reading/studying
2 unemployment increases when workers are replaced
3 impersonal contact, confinement to computer screens
4 computerised art becomes mechanical and impersonal - this isn't artistic
5 too much money/time spent on developing computers

Study Check 2

A Describe a visit to a street market where you bought an unusual object.

1 What kind of composition is this?
2 Which techniques are required for this topic?
3 Which paragraph plan should you follow?
4 How would you make your composition more interesting to the reader?
5 Is there a specific order of adjectives that you should follow in order to describe the object? If so, list the order.

B "I hope I'll never see him again." Write a story which begins or ends with these words.

1 In order to go back in time, which technique would you use in your story?
2 How can events be linked together in a story?
3 What style of language should you use?
4 Would you include descriptive techniques in your story? Why/Why not?
5 Which paragraph plan would you use in your story?

C On your way home after a football match you witnessed some hooligans smashing cars which were parked outside the stadium. Describe what happened.

1 Does this composition require narrative and descriptive techniques?
2 Which paragraph plan should you follow?
3 How can the events described be linked together?
4 Could you include hypotheses and evidence?

D Some friends of yours are thinking of moving to your area but they need some information first. Write a letter describing your area and pointing out the advantages of living there.

1 What kind of letter is this?
2 What aspects must be included in this letter?
3 What would the topic of each paragraph be?
4 How can you support the advantages?
5 Which opening and closing remarks can you include in your letter?

E "What is the correct way to bring up children?" Write a composition giving your opinion on this topic.

1 What kind of composition is this?
2 Which techniques can be used to begin and end your composition?
3 Which paragraph plan would you use?
4 Which linking words can be used in this type of composition?
5 Is it wrong to include a quotation?
6 Should you state your opinion in the introduction?

F Write a composition outlining the advantages and disadvantages of buying items from mail order catalogues.

1 What kind of composition is this?
2 What style of language should you use?
3 Is it necessary to make a list of the points for and against before writing your composition?
4 How can each point for or against be supported? Suggest points for or against.
5 Can you end this composition by giving a balanced consideration of the points?

G What can be done to reduce the amount of crime in our society?

1 What kind of composition is this?
2 What style of language should you use?
3 What is the paragraph plan that you will follow?
4 Which linking words will you use to connect suggestions and results?

UNIT 14 News Reports

1 **Read the following table, then listen to the cassette and fill in the missing information. Listen again, then retell the event in your own words.**

Time:	early **1)** ....
Place:	East Bristol
People involved:	one **2)** ....
Events:	• fire started on the **3)** .... floor of an abandoned **4)** .... • a passing **5)** .... spotted flames and **6)** .... the fire services • firemen fought the **7)** .... • firemen found a **8)** .... unconscious • he was taken to **9)** .... Hospital
Cause(s):	**10)** ....
Consequence(s):	fire **11)** .... the house
Comments:	"I've never seen a fire like this. The man's just **12)** .... to be alive."
Action taken:	the house will be **13)** .... next month

- A news report describes a particular event or topic which is of interest to the public. It is always written in a formal impersonal style and gives accurate facts only, not chatty descriptions. A good news report should consist of:
  - **a)** a **short eye-catching headline** which introduces the subject of the report;
  - **b)** an **introduction** which summarises the event giving information about the time, place and the people involved;
  - **c)** a **main body** consisting of two or more paragraphs in which the event is developed in detail. Information about the cause(s) and result(s) of the incident should also be included; and
  - **d)** a **conclusion** in which action to be taken or people's comments on the event are given.

  Such pieces of writing can be found in newspapers, magazines and newsletters.

Points to consider

- Give all necessary information accurately and in detail.
- Do not write about your feelings or your point of view concerning the incidents.
- Use passive voice and direct/reported speech to include people's comments and make the news report more interesting.

Introduction

Paragraph 1

summary of the event — time, place, people involved

Main Body

Paragraphs 2, 3, 4

description of the main events and people involved — give detailed facts

Conclusion

Final Paragraph

comments, reference to future developments

2 **Read the news report below and write down the topic of each paragraph, then underline all the words related to a car crash.**

Two seriously injured in car crash

Two people were seriously injured in a collision at the junction of Mill Road and Wrights Lane, Westbridge, early yesterday morning.

Jackie Hill, 22, was driving a yellow Nissan Cherry when she approached the junction and crashed into a delivery van coming out of Wrights Lane. A local resident who witnessed the accident said that it was obvious that Mrs Hill had not seen the stop sign at the junction as she had not even slowed down.

Mrs Hill was on her way home from her job as a night nurse when the accident happened. She is said to be in a serious but stable condition at St Michael's Hospital. The driver of the van, William Stephens, 27, is being treated for head and back injuries.

A neighbourhood association spokesman commented later: "This is the fourth accident to happen at the crossroads in the past month. We have been lobbying for a set of traffic lights there for months, but so far nothing has happened." According to city councillor David Wilkins, plans are being made to put up traffic lights at the junction in the near future.

Headlines are an important feature of news reports. They should both catch the reader's attention and inform the reader about the subject of the report. Since headlines must be short, words such as articles, parts of tenses, etc. are omitted. For example, instead of writing SOME ILLEGAL WEAPONS WERE FOUND IN AN ABANDONED FACTORY, the headline would read: ILLEGAL WEAPONS FOUND IN ABANDONED FACTORY.

3 **Write headlines for the following opening sentences of news reports. What do you think the reports go on to say?**

1 A bridge collapsed last Monday as a result of an earthquake which hit Southern California.

2 Last night's blackout has been traced to a mistake made by an employee at Peterville's central power plant. Engineer Harold Petty, 27, admitted having pushed the wrong button on a control panel.

3 Medical researchers in Britain say they may have found a cure for the common cold. In a series of controlled tests a combination of certain vitamins has been found to reduce symptoms dramatically.

4 It was announced yesterday that the planned motorway extension outside Peterfield will go ahead despite protests from environmental groups.

5 Two brothers who had gone missing three days before were found last night by a farmer, David Jones. They had been hiding in an abandoned barn on his property.

The style in which news reports are written differs in a number of ways from the style used in narratives (stories). A **narrative** is normally written in an informal, chatty style and calls for detailed descriptions, including the characters' feelings and sensations. Descriptive techniques can be employed to make the story more vivid. You can begin or end a narrative:

a) by describing weather, surroundings, people, etc. using the senses;
b) by using direct speech;
c) by addressing the reader (usually asking a question);
d) with a dramatic sentence creating mystery or suspense; or
e) by referring to your feelings or moods.

A **news report** is normally written in a formal style and deals only with detailed accurate facts. The writer's feelings are not mentioned. A news report starts with a summary of the event which is then developed in detail. To end a news report, we can mention people's comments using direct speech.

4 Match the beginnings with the endings, then decide which belong to news reports and which to stories, justifying your answers.

BEGINNINGS...

1 A hurricane hit northern Scotland yesterday morning, causing thousands of pounds worth of damage to buildings and littering the area with debris.

2 Underground workers remained on strike yesterday as negotiations with transport bosses broke down for the third time in two months.

3 "I don't know what we're going to do!" Cathy cried as she watched their boat drift further and further away. "Do you think anyone will find us?"

...ENDINGS

A As they sat by the fire, shivering with fear, they suddenly heard the distant sound of a motor. Bob jumped up, took a lighted branch from the fire and ran towards the beach. Help had come at last!

B "This is one of the worst natural disasters to hit the area for a long time," said the mayor of Thurso, one of the worst hit towns. Clean-up operations are already under way in an attempt to reduce the disruption caused by the damage.

C Transport authorities announced that they would be providing alternative means of transport for commuters, but long delays are expected at peak hours today.

5 Rewrite the following sentences in the passive.

1 Police finally caught convicted arsonist Thomas Wells early last Sunday morning. Prison guards found that Wells had escaped ten days earlier. Investigators believe that he has set two warehouses on fire since his escape.

2 The Council is providing temporary housing for citizens of Newton after Tuesday's flood damaged hundreds of homes. The location of the shelters is the nearby town of Holbrook, and authorities will allow the residents to stay in them until the Council rebuilds their homes.

3 Late Monday morning the police arrested two men who were selling stolen car stereo systems to unsuspecting customers. They seized all the stolen goods and are holding the men in custody.

6 **Read the following models, then decide which is a narrative and which is a news report, justifying your answers. Who was each model written by? Which person is each model written in? Give the paragraph plan, and suggest a headline/title for each model.**

MODEL A

Disabled swimmer Peter Carlton raced ahead of his opponents to take the gold medal in an incredible moment at yesterday's World Championship Watersports in Sydney. Carlton, a paraplegic, established a firm lead at the start of the race, his powerful arms more than making up for his weak legs. His final time was an impressive 1 minute 53 seconds which gave him the gold.

Carlton who was badly injured in a car crash in 1992, is a former world champion. The accident, however, left him in a wheelchair with almost no feeling or movement in either of his legs. Following three major operations, he was told by doctors that he would never swim competitively again.

Since that time Carlton has made amazing improvement under his trainer, Phil Stretton. His devotion to the sport made Carlton determined to prove the doctors wrong, and that determination has paid off.

"I'm ecstatic," Carlton told reporters after the race. "But the real credit for winning has to go to Phil, for his patience and faith in my ability."

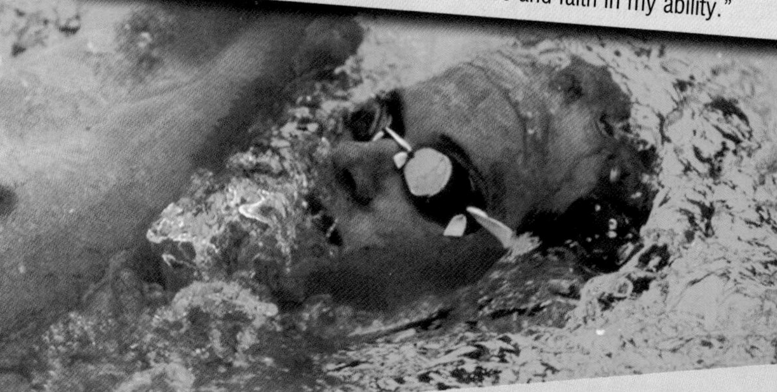

MODEL B

I heard the roar of the crowd, saw the constant flashing and clicking of cameras, felt water dripping down my back, and then I was being turned around and pushed towards the podium. On this slow motion journey, I began thinking about how familiar, and at the same time strange, all this was.

This time the faces weren't my manager's or trainer's - they were ambulancemen and nurses; the flashing wasn't cameras but police car lights; the liquid dripping was not from the swimming pool but blood from my own legs, and I was being carried on a stretcher towards the waiting ambulance.

Strangely enough, the worst moment wasn't the car accident itself, nor the pain, but when the doctor told me I wouldn't be doing very much swimming in the future. "What do you mean? What are you trying to tell me?" I yelled, knowing from his expression exactly what he meant. My resentment against that doctor — a man who didn't have the courage to tell me clearly that I would never swim or walk again — was such that I was determined to prove him wrong. And so I spent the next five years struggling against the odds, learning how to swim again with just my arms, fighting with those who said I couldn't and with myself when my body said I couldn't.

And now I'd done it. I'd won the World Championship, and I'd broken my own record. When I received the medal, I heard a voice from behind saying, "Congratulations! I suppose you don't remember me. I was your doctor about five years ago."

7 **Put the words listed below under the appropriate headline. Can you think of other related words? Now write a short news report about each one of the events.**

gun, security guard, flashing lights, country lane, silver spacecraft, hover above, cashier, staff, threaten to shoot, activate the alarm, strange whirring sound

A

BANK ROBBED OF MILLIONS

....

....

B

UFO SIGHTED

....

....

8 **Choose any two of the topics below and write in the appropriate style using 120 - 180 words.**

1. You work for a newspaper as a reporter. Write a news report about a missing child who was safely returned home. Now write the same topic as a narrative.
2. You work for a shipping newspaper. Write a news report about a ship that sank recently.
3. You have been asked to write a report on a car crash which cost the driver his life.

UNIT 15 Assessing Good and Bad Points

1 **A young couple has just returned from a package holiday and their travel agent has asked them to complete a questionnaire about the hotel they stayed at. Read the following questionnaire, then listen to the cassette and tick the appropriate boxes. Listen again and fill in the comments the couple made.**

Assessment of *Seaview* Hotel Guest(s) *Mr & Mrs Dummond*

Please tick (✔) the appropriate box.

	Excellent ☆☆☆☆	Good ☆☆☆	Average ☆☆	Poor ☆
Location	☐	☐	☐	☐
close to ...., shops on main road, a bit				
Facilities	☐	☐	☐	☐
two ...., swimming pool, no bars or				
Rooms	☐	☐	☐	☐
comfortable beds, big sitting area, big				
Service	☐	☐	☐	☐
room service: .... , reception and restaurant:				
Food	☐	☐	☐	☐
boring menu, food often .... and badly cooked				

General Comments: *not .... class, ... for holiday-makers, good .... for money*

A report assessing good and bad points is normally a formal piece of writing, and should consist of:

a) an **introduction** in which you state the purpose and content of your report;
b) a **main body** in which all information concerning the topic is presented in detail under sub-headings; and
c) a **final paragraph** which summarises the information mentioned in the main body, and states your opinion/recommendation.

Points to consider

- Before starting to write your report, think of who you are supposed to be according to the topic and who the report is addressed to. This will help you decide on the style of the report.
- Decide on the heading of the report, then carefully plan the information you will include. Decide on what you will write about, giving sub-headings, and think of what specific information you will include in each section.
- Use linking words to join your ideas. If you feel there are negative aspects to be mentioned, present them under the relevant sub-headings, as well as the positive aspects. Join the positive and negative comments using appropriate words (**however, nevertheless, on the other hand, in contrast,** etc).
- Present tenses are normally used in this kind of report. However, past tenses are used for reports related to past events, *e.g. a report about a restaurant.*

Useful language

To introduce: As requested, The purpose/aim of this report is to ..., etc.
To make contrasting points: However, Although, Despite, But, While, Even though, etc.
To express the difference between appearance and reality: It may seem, On the surface, Apparently, etc.
To conclude/summarise: On the whole, In conclusion, To conclude, To sum up, etc.

Introduction

state the purpose and content of your report

Main Body

summarise each point under suitable sub-headings, giving both positive and negative points (if any)

Conclusion

general assessment and/or recommendation

2 **You have been asked to visit a place with a view to using it for receptions, and to write a report about it. Read the model report and answer the following questions: a) What information is given about the location, services and security? b) Is Oakley Hall recommended or not? c) What tenses have been used? Finally, list the good and bad points in the table below.**

To: Mrs Rollins, Foreign Affairs Officer
From: David Stern, Administrative Assistant
Subject: Oakley Hall

Introduction

The purpose of this report is to assess the suitability of Oakley Hall for hosting formal receptions in honour of visiting foreign officials.

Location and Features

Oakley Hall is located on King Street, only three kilometres from the Embassy. The two-acre grounds are well-kept and attractive. The three-storey building consists of a large reception hall on the second floor and a smaller function room on the first floor. The larger hall can accommodate 300 people, while the smaller hall on the first floor can accommodate 150. Although there is a garden behind the building, outdoor receptions are not available.

Services

Oakley Hall has a staff of 100 and offers a wide range of services. The kitchen serves international cuisine and the bar includes a wide variety of wines. Waiting staff, bartenders and parking attendants are also available for receptions; please note that an extra fee will be charged for these services.

Security

Oakley Hall is surrounded by a high wrought-iron fence and all entrances are observed by security cameras. There are guards positioned at the main and rear gates. The car park, located outside the gates, is also guarded. Although this may seem adequate, the area along the fence must also be patrolled to prevent trespassers from entering the grounds.

Recommendations

In conclusion, it is recommended that Oakley Hall be used for our receptions. It satisfies all our requirements and as far as security measures are concerned, they can easily be improved to suit our needs.

Good Points	Bad Points

3 **Join the sentences with appropriate linking words.**

1 The amusement park has several exciting rides which are included in the entrance fee. Some are not suitable for young children or the elderly.
2 There is a wide variety of shops in the airport terminal. They tend to charge extremely high prices.
3 The food served at the restaurant is healthy and reasonably priced. It can taste rather bland at times.
4 Classes at the language school are small and well taught. Many students feel that they are not given enough individual attention.

4 **As head of a department you have been asked by the company manager to comment on an *employee's performance as he is being considered for promotion.* Look at your draft notes and fill in the appropriate linking words from the lists. Then, using your notes, write your report.**

To: Michael Adams, Manager
From: John McDonald, Department Head
Subject: Work performance of Peter Thompson

Introduction

The purpose of this report is to assess the work performance of Peter Thompson, who is currently being considered for promotion.

Customer Relations

***a)** also - although - however*

- usually polite and cheerful; has rarely been the subject of customer complaints
- ...., helpful and sociable; has a good approach when dealing with customers
- there have, ..., been times when he has been rather aggressive, ... this is not his usual manner

....

Staff Relations

***b)** in addition to - on the other hand - as well*

- he has recently been assisting with the training of new personnel; has been the staff representative ...., so he knows how to deal with difficulties
- .... being highly motivated, he also motivates other employees
- ...., he can be stubborn and will stop at nothing to persuade others he is right
- he is respected and popular with the staff; works well with other people

....

Conclusion

***c)** but also - not only - to sum up*

- he would be valuable addition to management team; he .... knows all levels of business, ... relates well to other staff members
- ...., he is an excellent candidate for promotion

....

5 **Read the following report and divide it into suitable paragraphs. What sub-headings could you use for each paragraph? How does this report finish?**

To: Jane Hickson, Editor, *New Gourmet* magazine
From: James Ritchie, Staff Reporter
Subject: Bailey's Restaurant, 18 Spring Street

As requested, this is my assessment report on Bailey's Restaurant, where a friend and I had dinner on Saturday night. The restaurant occupies the ground floor of a beautiful Regency terraced house. With a seating capacity of 70 people, it has deep carpets, soft lighting from wall-mounted lamps, and rich oak panelling on the walls. The effect is both luxurious and welcoming. The menu offers traditional British cooking, as well as a few French and Italian dishes. I chose roast beef as a main course, and my companion had lamb. Although the food was well cooked and attractively presented, I felt the choice of starters and desserts was very limited. Despite the fact that the restaurant was completely full on Saturday, the service was reasonably quick. The waiters and waitresses were all polite and efficient. The bill, for a three-course meal for two people, with a bottle of wine, was £85. There are several dishes on the menu which are far more expensive than the ones we chose, and these prices are rather high for the quality of food served. To sum up, Bailey's Restaurant has an attractive décor and a pleasant atmosphere, as well as good food and service. However, the menu is limited and on the whole our dinner was certainly overpriced.

6 **As a writer for a consumer advice magazine, you have been asked to write an assessment report on a local supermarket which is part of a large national chain.**

i) Read the following comments which customers have made about the supermarket and use them to complete the table below.

They have lots of very cheap special offers.

There isn't a very wide choice of different brands.

It's nice to be able to do all your shopping in one place.

Their normal prices aren't much cheaper than the prices at other supermarkets.

The way they've arranged the shelves makes it easy to find what you want.

You can save a lot of money by buying their "own brand" of goods.

It's quite a long way from the town centre, and it's hard to find a parking space.

There are lots of different sections – a meat counter, a bakery, a cosmetics counter and things like that – so you can get everything you need.

They have thousands and thousands of different products.

Good Points	Bad Points

ii) Choose three of the following headings to include in your report.

- Décor, atmosphere
- Variety of products
- Facilities for children
- Prices
- Comfort
- Convenience

iii) Now write your report in a formal style. Remember to include an introduction, conclusion, and linking words.

7 **Go through the following topics and decide on appropriate headings and sub-headings, then give the paragraph plan for each. Finally, write any two of them using 120-180 words.**

1 You are working for a travel agency and have been asked to visit the Hotel Belluncia to decide if it is appropriate for family holidays. Write a report for the company.

2 The kindergarten school you work for has asked you to visit a local leisure centre with a view to taking the children there for the day. Write a report for the school.

3 You are a teacher and you spent three weeks last summer accompanying students from your school on a language course at a British college. The Dean of the college has asked you to write a report assessing the course and the facilities on campus. Write a report for the college.

UNIT 16 Survey Reports

1 Listen to these two people talking about a survey and fill in the missing percentages. What are they talking about?

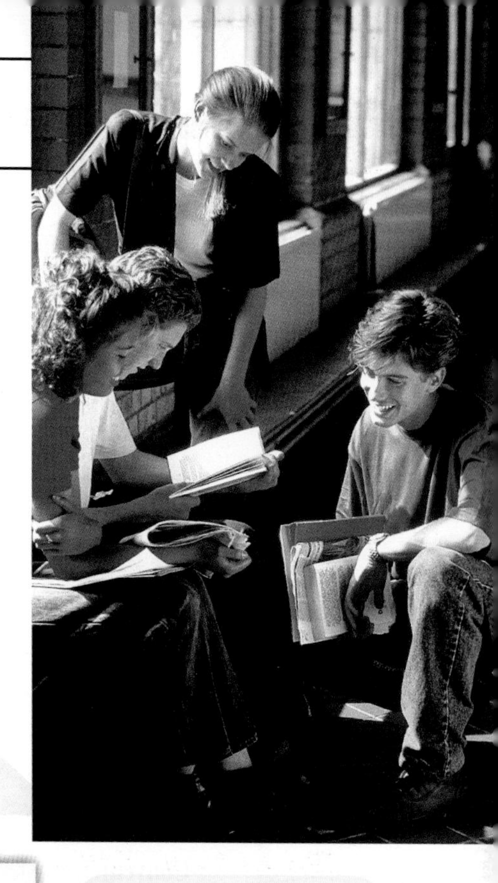

A survey report is normally a formal piece of writing based on research. It may be less formal depending who it is addressed to, e.g. a friend. A good survey report should consist of:

a) an **introduction** in which you state the purpose and content of your report;

b) a **main body** in which all information collected on the topic is presented in detail. You can use sub-headings, numbers or letters to separate each piece of information; and

c) a **conclusion** in which you summarise all points mentioned before. Your recommendation or suggestion(s) can be included as well.

Points to consider

- Before starting your report, consider who you are supposed to be, according to the topic, and who the report is addressed to. This will help you decide on the style of the report. *e.g. You work for a travel agency. Your boss has asked you to write a report ...* This means you are an employee in a travel agency and that your report will be addressed to your boss; therefore it should be formal in style.
- Decide on the main heading of the report, then carefully plan the information you will include in your report and divide it into sub-headings.
- Present tenses should be used in survey reports to introduce generalisations. Use a variety of reporting verbs such as: *state, report, agree, claim, complain,* etc., to introduce reported speech.
- Use expressions such as: *one in five, seven out of ten, thirty per cent of the people questioned, the majority of those questioned, a large proportion of, a minority of,* etc. to report the results of the survey.
- Facts may be supported by generalisations. *e.g. Fifty-five per cent of young people go to the cinema at least twice a month. (fact) This indicates that the cinema is still quite a popular form of entertainment among young people. (generalisation)*

Useful Language for Survey Reports

To introduce: The purpose/aim of this report, As requested, This survey was carried out
To generalise: In general, Generally, On the whole
To introduce other people's opinions: Many people consider, Some people argue/believe/ claim
To conclude/summarise: In conclusion, All things considered, To sum up, All in all

Introduction

state purpose and content of your report

Development

summarise your information under suitable sub-headings

Conclusion

end with a general conclusion and, if necessary, make recommendations or suggestions

2 **Read the following report and write down the topic of each paragraph. Is the style formal or less formal? What questions do you think were asked in the survey?**

To: *James Lawton, Council Representative*
From: *Jane Sigmund*
Subject: *Public satisfaction with local underground railway system*

purpose - content (500 people questioned about local underground system)

Purpose
The aim of this report is to analyse the results of a survey in which 500 residents were questioned about the local underground railway system and whether or not they were satisfied with it.

Convenience
Many people do not find the system convenient. This is illustrated by the fact that more than fifty per cent complained that stations are too far from their homes and that there are not enough trains. There were also complaints that the system can only be used to reach a few areas of the city, forcing many customers to use other means of public transport to complete their journeys.

Cost
Seventy per cent of those questioned had no complaints about the cost of the service. This shows that the majority of passengers consider the cost reasonable, and that a slight increase would be considered acceptable.

Comfort
A large number of people who participated in the survey stated that they felt the trains are insufficiently heated in cold weather. There were also comments on the hardness of the seats and that trains are not always as clean as they might be. This indicates that passengers are not entirely satisfied as far as comfort is concerned.

Recommendation
All points considered, some improvements evidently need to be made if passengers are to be satisfied with the service. Perhaps a slight increase in the fare would make it possible for the service to be improved in the areas mentioned in this report.

3 **Look back at the diagram on page 91. Use the expressions below to complete the sentences about the results of the survey regarding young people's reading preferences.**

minority, a small number, a reasonable number, majority, per cent, by far the largest, two in four

1 Slightly more than .... of those surveyed prefer reading magazines.
2 A .... of young people surveyed read comics in their free time.
3 .... of young people choose to read non-fiction.
4 .... of those surveyed read fiction.
5 Only eight .... of the people surveyed prefer to read non-fiction.
6 The .... of the young people surveyed read magazines.
7 .... number of those surveyed read magazines.

Survey reports include facts and generalisations.

- **Facts** can be presented in the form of **percentages** *(ten per cent, two in ten, three out of ten,* etc) or **proportions** *(the majority/minority, a significant number, a large/the largest proportion, by far, a small number, etc.)*
- **Generalisations** are statements which help clarify the facts. They can either precede or come after facts. Depending on this position, facts and generalisations can be linked by using verbs either in their active or passive form, as shown in the examples:*e.g. Only twenty per cent of students take post-graduate courses. This* ***indicates/illustrates/ implies/shows*** *that most students prefer to pursue a career rather than to continue their studies.* **or** *Most students prefer to pursue a career rather than continue their studies. This* ***is indicated/illustrated/ implied/shown*** *by the fact that only twenty per cent take post-graduate courses.*

4 **Read the extracts and decide which sentences present facts and which present generalisations. Then link them using one of the ways mentioned above.**

1 Fifty-eight per cent of those who go on tropical holidays are high-earning professionals. They are able to spend more on their holidays than the average person.

....

2 Young people enjoy holidays which involve outdoor activities. A significant number of students spend their money on adventure holidays.

....

3 Two in three families with young children take package holidays. Parents like to take advantage of the fact that they do not have to organise their holidays themselves.

....

4 Older people like to go on holidays that are quiet and relaxing. Sixty-three per cent of holidaymakers who go on cruises are over the age of fifty.

....

5 A small proportion of people prefer camping holidays. Few people wish to spend their holidays without basic facilities.

....

5 **Read the following sentences which talk about eating out. Which belong to a formal report?**

1 Fifteen per cent of those surveyed stated that they did not mind how much they spent on a good meal out.
2 Lots of young people go to fast food places because the atmosphere's lively and they can meet their friends there.
3 Nearly half of those questioned said they ate at Indian restaurants because it is a convenient alternative to cooking at home.
4 It's great to be waited on hand and foot – the waiters treat you like a king.
5 The majority of those surveyed chose to eat fast food because of the wide variety of food to choose from.
6 The curries are excellent – the whole family enjoys having a meal there.

6 **Fill in the diagram with information from Ex. 5, then, using your notes write a report in a formal style. Use your own ideas as well.**

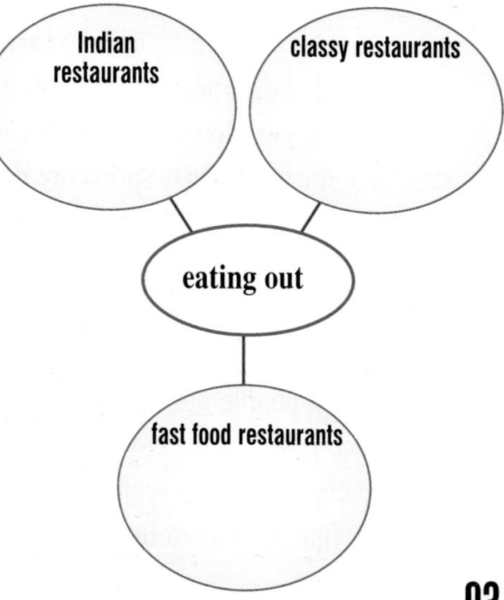

7 **Read the following report and fill in suitable headings. What style is it written in?**

From: Carol Sullivan
To: Paul Barnes
Subject: Children's Toys

....

The aim of this report is to outline the results of a survey which was carried out to assess the popularity of the various types of toys sold at Toy City. Five hundred children aged between five and fourteen were questioned.

....

Currently only twenty per cent of stock consists of computer and electronic games; however, the survey indicated that these were by far the most popular purchases. This is shown by the fact that over forty per cent of those questioned were buying such items.

....

Traditional toys aimed specifically at boys or girls make up fifty per cent of stock at the moment, but our survey suggests a fairly significant decrease in the popularity of such toys. This is demonstrated by the fact that only thirty per cent of those surveyed were buying these kinds of toys.

....

A further thirty per cent of those surveyed were purchasing miscellaneous items ranging from board games to rubber snakes. The fact that such toys constitute approximately thirty per cent of stock suggests that there has been little change in their popularity.

....

To sum up, it seems that the most popular items in Toy City are computer and electronic games. For this reason, it is suggested that we increase our stock of these games while reducing the percentage of traditional toys aimed specifically at boys or girls.

8 ***Your pen-friend has asked you to write a report about how young people in your country entertain themselves.*** **Read the report and punctuate it. Is it formal or less formal? Into which sections can it be divided?**

in my country young people have various options for entertaining themselves during the holidays and at weekends many young people relax with friends or might even go window-shopping on cold days they usually go to the cinema or stay at home watching tv sports are popular football and swimming for example are widely enjoyed as most districts have excellent facilities with reduced rates for students evenings out are often spent at a bar most young people enjoy playing a game of darts and chatting with their friends occasionally they visit a night club or disco attending a rock concert is another favourite outing some young people are also keen on the arts and take advantage of theatre and dance performances since there is a great variety of forms of entertainment to choose from it seems that everyone decides to enjoy themselves the way they find suits them the most

9 **Write one of the topics below in the appropriate style using 120-180 words.**

1 Your teacher has asked you to conduct a survey into the reasons why people decide to learn a foreign language. Write a report analysing the results of the survey.
2 You work for a fitness magazine which has recently conducted a survey into the popularity of various forms of exercise. Write a report analysing the results of the survey.
3 Your pen-friend has asked you to write a short report on the eating habits of young people in your country to include in his report for his school project. Write a report for your pen-friend.

UNIT 17 Reporting Experiences

1 **You are going to hear a student giving a talk to his language school class about a trip he recently took. First read the table below, then listen to the cassette and tick the appropriate boxes.**

1 The trip took place at:

the end of summer ☐	the beginning of autumn ☐	Christmas ☐

2 The reason for the trip was:

to have an unusual holiday ☐	to attend a conference ☐	to study ☐

3 The student went to:

Brazil ☐	India ☐	Egypt ☐

4 What did the student do each day?

Day One:	boat trip ☐	desert trip ☐	visit to museum ☐
Day Two:	tour of city ☐	visit to Great Pyramid ☐	bus ride ☐
Day Three:	sightseeing ☐	relaxation at lake ☐	train trip ☐
Day Four:	shopping ☐	visit to traditional market ☐	visit to museum ☐
Day Five:	visit to museum ☐	visit to palace ☐	day trip to Luxor ☐

5 The student feels that the trip was:

a great experience ☐	only worthwhile for someone with a special interest ☐
too boring ☐	

When you are asked to report experiences, you normally write in an informal style. Such reports should consist of:

a) an **introduction** in which you state the topic of your report, giving information about the event, date and people involved;

b) a **main body** in which all information (events) is presented in chronological order in various sections (these sections can be indicated by using sub-headings); and

c) a **conclusion** in which you summarise your points and refer to your feelings, moods or consequences.

This kind of writing can be found in newspapers or magazines in article form, or as part of a letter to a friend.

Points to consider

- Before starting your report, think of who you are supposed to be and who the report is addressed to. This will help you decide on the style of the report.
- Decide on the events you will include in your report and divide them into paragraphs under suitable sub-headings. Alternatively, you can use numbers or letters.
- Join your sentences using appropriate linking words or time expressions.
- Past tenses are used in reports of this kind.

Introduction

state topic and set the scene (what-when-where-who-why)

Main Body

information in chronological order under suitable sub-headings

Conclusion

summarise points, refer to feelings/moods/consequences

2 **The model below is based on the topic** ***"You went to England during the summer for a short language course. When you returned to your local language school, you were asked to write a report on your experiences for the school newsletter."*** **Read the model and write down the topic of each paragraph. Is it formal or informal? Underline the time words used. What tenses have been used? Why?**

In July, I went to England for a three-week language course at Wellington College, Crowthorne. There were fifty students on the course, from more than a dozen different countries.

Arrival

Two teachers met me when I arrived at Heathrow, and they introduced me to some of the other students. Then we went to the school by coach, and unpacked in our dormitories – big rooms with beds for six students. After that we went to the dining hall for our first English meal, which was fish and chips.

The School Days

The next day we had three hours of English lessons, and after lunch we went riding. I had never been on a horse before, but it was great! That evening I watched TV while some of the other students played table tennis or listened to music. Most days followed this pattern, although I also tried canoeing as well as playing tennis and football.

Excursions

At the end of the first week, we went to Howlett's Zoo. The zoo-keeper let us feed the gorillas, but some of the students were too scared to go near them! We went on excursions to Dover and Margate, too, and on the last weekend we went up to London where we went sightseeing and bought presents for our friends and family.

Farewell

On the last evening of the course, we had a disco. One of the teachers was the DJ, so he played all the songs we liked. The next morning I said goodbye to all my new friends, and went home. I had a wonderful time, and I want to go back next year. I think my English has improved, too!

WELLINGTON COLLEGE

WELLINGTON COLLEGE

3 *Your school presents an annual concert of music and dance, produced and performed by students. You were a member of the production committee for last year's concert, and have been asked for a report on your experience in order to help this year's committee prepare for the event.* **Read the report below, punctuate it correctly and give a one-word sub-heading for each section.**

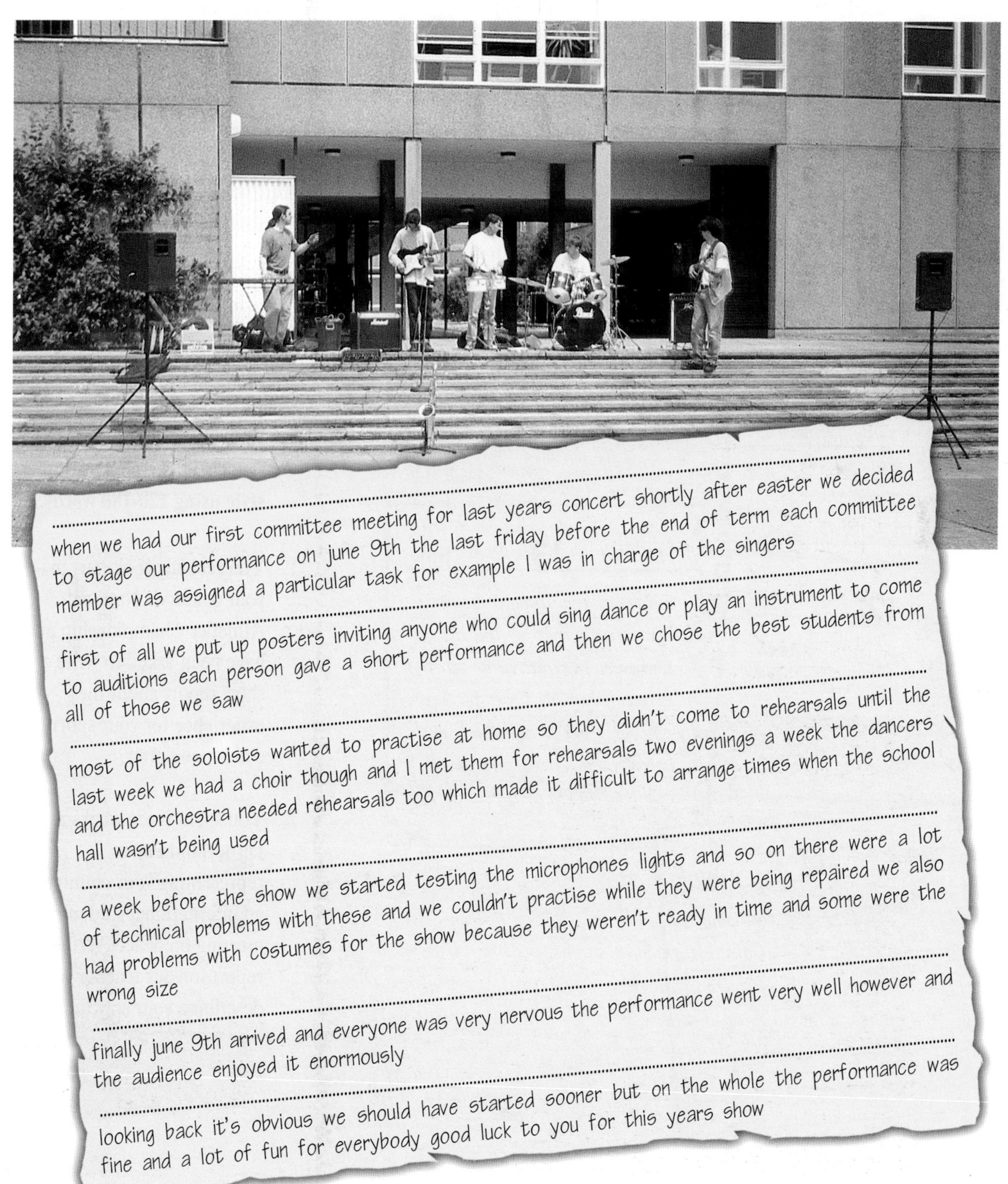

....

when we had our first committee meeting for last years concert shortly after easter we decided to stage our performance on june 9th the last friday before the end of term each committee member was assigned a particular task for example I was in charge of the singers

....

first of all we put up posters inviting anyone who could sing dance or play an instrument to come to auditions each person gave a short performance and then we chose the best students from all of those we saw

....

most of the soloists wanted to practise at home so they didn't come to rehearsals until the last week we had a choir though and I met them for rehearsals two evenings a week the dancers and the orchestra needed rehearsals too which made it difficult to arrange times when the school hall wasn't being used

....

a week before the show we started testing the microphones lights and so on there were a lot of technical problems with these and we couldn't practise while they were being repaired we also had problems with costumes for the show because they weren't ready in time and some were the wrong size

....

finally june 9th arrived and everyone was very nervous the performance went very well however and the audience enjoyed it enormously

....

looking back it's obvious we should have started sooner but on the whole the performance was fine and a lot of fun for everybody good luck to you for this years show

4 **You went to Toronto for five days to attend your sister's wedding. Look at the extracts from the diary you kept during your trip there and match them with the headings. Then write your report on the trip.**

5 **Write either of the following reports in the appropriate style using 120-180 words.**

1 You recently took part in your country's National Athletics Championship and have been asked to write a short report about the experience for your sports club's newsletter.

2 You spent three weeks at Disneyland Paris representing your country at an international students' meeting on peace. Write a report to your teacher describing your stay there.

UNIT 18 Articles

1 **Listen to the beginning of these articles and match them with the headlines. Which articles are formal and which are informal? What techniques would you use to write them?**

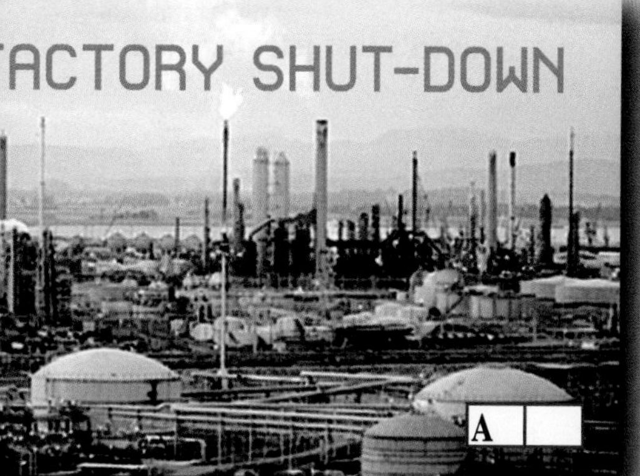

Articles are written to give information (e.g. news reports) or express opinions (e.g. argumentative articles). They can be either formal or informal depending on the audience they are addressed to and the topic they deal with. A good article consists of:

a) an eye-catching **headline** which suggests the topic of the article that follows;
b) an interesting **introduction**;
c) a **main body** consisting of two or more paragraphs in which the topic is presented in detail; and
d) a **conclusion** which gives an appropriate ending to the article.

Such pieces of writing can be found in newspapers, magazines or newsletters.

Points to consider

- Decide on the style of the article before you start writing.
- Always think of a short, clear, appropriate headline which attracts the reader's interest.
- Each paragraph should deal with one aspect of the topic. You can use linking ideas or time expressions to join your ideas or introduce paragraphs.
- Avoid using simplistic adjectives (good, nice, bad, etc). Always try to use more sophisticated vocabulary instead. *(splendid, gorgeous, awful, etc)*
- Address the reader in the second person (you) if the topic of the article and the style you have adopted permits this.
- Descriptive, narrative and argumentative techniques - as presented in previous units (units 1, 2, 4, 6, 10, 11, 12, 13) - can be applied when writing articles.

2 **Match these headlines with the topics below. There are two headlines for each topic. Which are the most successful? Why?**

a **Exams not necessary**
b Tahiti: Holidaymaker's paradise
c **The ferry ran onto rocks**
d **Exams to be banned?**
e **Go to Tahiti for your holidays**
f Storm forces ferry onto rocks

1 You are a reporter for a newspaper. Write an article about a ferry boat which ran aground in rough seas.
2 Your school magazine has asked its readers to give their opinions on whether exams are useful as a means of testing students' knowledge. Write your article.
3 You are a reporter for a weekly magazine. Write an article describing a popular holiday resort.

How to Write Headlines for News Articles

A headline is a short, clear summary of the information presented in a newspaper article. To write headlines correctly, certain rules must be followed.

a) use the **present simple** tense to describe events which have occurred very recently. *Earthquake **hits** L.A.*, for example, means the earthquake has just happened, probably in the last twenty-four hours;

b) omit the verb "be" when using the passive voice to describe a past event. Write: *President defeated* or *Lost boy found* not: *President was defeated* or *Lost boy was found*;

c) write "to be + past participle" when using the passive voice to describe a future event, as in: *Hospital to be opened by Queen (= A hospital is going to be opened by the Queen.)* When using the active voice to describe a future event, write the full infinitive (to be) only, as in *Queen to open hospital (= The Queen is going to open a hospital);*

d) omit articles (a, an, the) as in *Child trapped in rubble (= A child was trapped in rubble)*;

e) put nouns one after the other as in *London factory explosion injures 27* (which means that an explosion in a factory located in London resulted in twenty-seven people being injured;

f) avoid using prepositions (words like **under, over, across, through**). Write: *Unidentified virus spreads* rather than *An unidentified virus has spread across the country)*; and

g) use abbreviations like US, UN, NATO. Write: *UFO sighted* not: *An unidentified flying object was seen.*

3 Try to rewrite the following sentences into headlines, applying the theory above.

1 The prisoners' protest at the Tryall jail has ended.

....

2 Banks are planning to introduce security cameras at cashpoint machines.

....

3 A tanker overturned, spilling its cargo of heating oil on the M11 motorway.

....

4 Nutritionists have condemned new slimming drugs as very harmful.

....

5 The London School of Economics has won an award for being the best business school.

....

6 The Organisation of Petroleum Exporting Countries has made a deal to fix oil prices.

....

7 The Zolosis factory was blamed for failing to protect workers against unsafe chemical levels.

....

8 Contaminated baby food of various brands has caused a scare in the city of Redding.

....

9 The director of the car company will be charged with fraud.

....

4 Look at the following headlines and expand them into proper sentences.

1 **Queen's lost jewels found**

2 Collision kills five

3 **Manchester wins cup**

4 **Explosion destroys factory**

5 **Prince to wed**

6 Dustmen's strike over

7 **Election called by PM**

8 7.5 quake kills 5000

9 **Scandal threatens government**

10 Hospital to be closed

11 **War declared**

12 Storm destroys corn crop

13 **Terrorist drama ends peacefully**

14 **Clinton, Pope to meet**

15 **UN Warning: starvation in Africa**

5 **Read the following sentences, underline the key words, then write possible headlines.**

1 Breston is becoming a busy holiday resort due to the Mayor's successful promotional campaign.
2 A mother of four won £1 million in the national lottery last week.
3 A massive earthquake has destroyed most of Clifford Bay. Forty people were killed and fifty are still missing.
4 An attempt was made on the French Ambassador's life while he was visiting Austria. The assassin, who failed in his mission, was arrested.
5 Sting is going to give a concert in London. All proceeds from the concert will go to Amnesty International.
6 Medical researchers have discovered a new treatment which will help people suffering from asthma.
7 Many teachers object to the introduction of computers in school education, as they fear that computers will eventually replace them.
8 Police seized drugs worth £1,000,000 at London's Heathrow airport last Monday.

6 **Read the following article and give the paragraph outline. Is it formal or informal? Where would you be likely to find this article?**

Massive earthquake hits Georgia

A devastating earthquake measuring 8.2 on the Richter scale struck the provincial town of Brozhomi in Georgia, Southern Russia, last night.

Residents were awakened shortly after 2.00 am by violent tremors lasting more than a minute. Eighty people were killed in the earthquake, which destroyed hundreds of homes and caused severe damage to those left standing.

Authorities fear that dozens of people may still be trapped under the debris of ruined buildings. Rescue efforts have been hampered by a lack of equipment, and rescue workers are battling under appalling weather conditions in subzero temperatures.

Speaking over the wail of sirens, Vasya Puchka described her personal tragedy. "There is nothing left for me. I have lost my home, my husband and three young children. I saw them die."

Unable to cope with the widespread devastation, Georgia has appealed to the international community for medical supplies and help with temporary housing. The rest of the world has been quick to respond. Fleets of trucks carrying food, medical supplies and tents are already on their way in an attempt to relieve the horrific situation.

7 **Match the beginnings and endings below, then decide on an appropriate headline for each pair. Which of the sets are informal and which are formal? What does each set talk about? Where could each article be found?**

BEGINNINGS...

1 If you're looking for an exciting holiday, let me recommend the Florida Keys. It's the ideal place for both fun and relaxation.

2 In the recent past, Olympic medal winners have been accused of taking drugs to enhance their performance. They have even been stripped of their titles after drug tests have come out positive. Why are athletes taking drugs?

3 A whale was safely returned to the sea yesterday after spending two days stranded in shallow waters on the coast of Brenton, North Devon. Dozens of villagers joined in the rescue effort and, with the use of special equipment, moved the whale into deeper waters.

...ENDINGS

A At a press conference today, Deborah Adams, Chief Marine Biologist at Millford Aquarium, thanked all those who had helped, saying it "couldn't have been done without them." The whale is being monitored and appears to be in good condition.

B The Florida Keys is a place I'll always remember. Why don't you try it for yourselves this year?

C All in all, it appears to be a combination of pressure to be the best, the will to win and fear of failure, which can become a deadly cocktail. Some athletes cannot cope and find themselves pushed to their limits. It is then that they turn to the easy, illegal option.

8 **Read the following article and replace the words in bold with adjectives from the list below. What headline would you suggest for the article? What techniques have been used?**

confident - depressing - dramatic - enormous - enthusiastic - gleaming - inadequate - inspiring - magnificent - wonderful

The Queen Mother officially opened the **1) nice** new £200m Children's Wing of St Bernadette's Hospital in London yesterday, to the **2) happy** cheers of medical staff and representatives of the charity which raised the money for the project.

Gone is the **3) sad** old Children's Wing, built in 1820, with its **4) bad** facilities and ugly brick walls; in its place is a(n) **5) clean** new structure with 500 beds, 4 operating theatres and state-of-the-art equipment.

This **6) big** change is thanks to the efforts of the Children's Hospital Fund, a charity organisation which raised the £200m needed to build the new wing when spending cuts made it necessary to close the old block. A hospital spokesman thanked the charity on behalf of sick children everywhere and said he was **7) sure** that St Bernadette's could now offer medical treatment "to rival that of any hospital in the world."

In her speech, the Queen Mother said, "The **8) great** efforts of the Children's Hospital Fund are a (n) **9) good** example to us all and will make a(n) **10) big** difference to the lives of thousands of children, now and for generations to come."

9 **Read the article below. Then read the topic sentences and put them in the right box. Where do you think this article is taken from?**

JOIN IN RECYCLING SCHEMES

Have you ever really stopped to think about how much rubbish you and your family throw away? Every day we produce incredible amounts of waste. If we don't do something about it, we are in danger of turning this whole planet into a gigantic rubbish dump. Throwing away rubbish also means we are throwing away our planet's precious resources.

1 [ ] Aluminium cans are the perfect example. It costs less to recycle an aluminium can than to make a new one, and ***one*** person recycling ***one*** can a day would save 50 litres of petrol every year.

2 [ ] Take advantage of recycling facilities in your city. You can divide your rubbish into different bags for glass, metal, plastics and paper, so these can be handled separately.

3 [ ] After all, it's true what they say: "If you're not part of the solution, you're part of the problem."

a Recycling is easy, but we all have to play a part instead of leaving it to someone else.

b So what can be done? Recycling is the answer.

c There's no excuse for just throwing away your rubbish.

10 **Read the following opening paragraphs and decide which are formal and which are informal, then write an appropriate headline. Finally, give the paragraph plan and complete the articles.**

1 Want to escape from the monotony of daily life? Go to Monaco, with its luxurious hotels, 16th century palace and magnificent cathedral. Have cash to spare? Go to one of the famous casinos and try your luck. But don't overdo it.

2 At a time when pollution is at its worst, governments are working on plans to find ways to reduce the problem. One suggestion being considered is to introduce free public transport in major European cities. This would certainly be one way of tackling the pollution which is slowly choking city dwellers.

3 Twenty-three football supporters were seriously injured at yesterday's Cup Final as a security fence collapsed on spectators in the west stand. Overcrowding and lack of police control were blamed for the tragedy.

4 Colourful floats, spectacular costumes, streets brightly decorated with balloons and streamers – here you are in Rio, enjoying the famous carnival. This is the most amazing carnival in the world and surely one of the most unforgettable experiences you'll ever have.

Revision Box

11 **Mark the statements True or False justifying your answers.**

1 Articles should always be written in formal style. ☐
2 Articles should not include narrative techniques. ☐
3 Addressing the reader is a way of keeping his/her interest. ☐
4 Articles should always have a headline. ☐
5 More sophisticated adjectives should be avoided. ☐

12 **Read the following topics, identify the style they require and suggest an appropriate headline and a paragraph plan. Then write any two of them using 120-180 words.**

1 Your school magazine has asked students to give their opinion on whether computers should be used in the classroom.
2 A young people's magazine has asked its readers to write an article promoting the most famous holiday resort in their country.
3 The newspaper you are working for has asked you to write an article on a recent disaster which hit the capital of your country.
4 A health and diet magazine has asked its readers to write an article giving their opinion on junk food.

UNIT 19 Reviews

1 **Look at the table below, then listen to the cassette and tick the appropriate boxes.**

Name of film to be seen:	Robin Hood ☐	Rob Roy ☐	
Type of film:	thriller ☐	comedy ☐	adventure ☐
Star(s):	Liam Neeson ☐	Kevin Costner ☐	Morgan Freeman ☐
Story theme:	someone's efforts to help the poor ☐	a Scottish hero and his wife ☐	
Acting:	powerful ☐	poor ☐	excellent ☐
Plot:	dramatic ☐	gripping ☐	confusing ☐
Characters:	well-developed ☐	predictable ☐	weak ☐
Recommendation:	waste of time and money ☐	not to be missed ☐	

A review is a short description of a film, play, book, etc. It is either formal or informal in style, depending on the readers it is addressed to. Present tenses are normally used in a review. A good review should consist of:

a) an **introduction** in which you give all the background information of the story (setting, type, characters, etc);

b) a **main body** consisting of two paragraphs in which all the main points of the plot are presented in time sequence as well as comments on acting, plot, character development, directing, etc.;

c) a **conclusion** in which the writer recommends or does not recommend the film/book/performance etc, giving reasons.

Useful Language for Reviews

Background: This well-written/informative/ fascinating book ..., The film/story is set in ..., The film/book tells the story of ..., This work is based on ..., etc.
Main points of plot: The plot focuses on ..., The story begins ..., The plot has an unexpected twist ..., The film reaches a dramatic climax ..., etc.
General comments: It is rather long/confusing/slow etc, The cast is excellent/weak ..., The script is dull/clever ..., It has a tragic/surprising end ..., etc.
Recommendations: Don't miss it, it will change the way you see ..., It is well worth seeing ..., I wouldn't recommend it because ..., etc.

Introduction

Paragraph 1

background (setting, type of story, main characters)

Main Body

Paragraph 2

main points of the plot

Paragraph 3

general comments

Conclusion

Paragraph 4

recommendation

2 **Read the model and write down the topic of each paragraph.**

"DENNIS THE MENACE"

Dennis the Menace is a comedy set in a quiet American neighbourhood. Mason Gable plays the lead role as Dennis, the 8-year-old mischief-maker who manages to catch a thief. Walter Matthau is Mr Wilson, the man who lives next door to Dennis.

A thief steals gold coins from Mr Wilson and, as he's running away, he spots Dennis hiding in Mr Wilson's garden. Dennis is snatched by the thief and their adventure begins. Dennis is not the least bit frightened and drives the thief mad with his constant talking. Soon he discovers that the thief has Mr Wilson's gold. The film reaches a humorous climax when Dennis ties the thief up and hands him over to the police. Mr Wilson then sees Dennis in a different light.

The cast is excellent, and young Mason Gable surely has a bright acting career ahead of him. The film is full of hilarious scenes as it successfully portrays children's natural curiosity in a comical way.

Dennis the Menace is a film well worth seeing. Children of all ages, as well as adults, will love this charming story. It is a highly entertaining film which is sure to be one of the year's biggest hits.

3 **The following lists of adjectives are used to describe plot, script and characters. List them in the appropriate boxes.**

A ***moving, confusing, original, well-written, thrilling, tragic, highly entertaining, gripping, excellent, shocking, poorly-written, involving, unimaginative***

PLOT/STORY
SCRIPT

B ***well-developed, boring, strong, humorous, realistic, weak, dull, convincing, predictable, unbelievable, frightening***

CHARACTERS	
POSITIVE	NEGATIVE

4 **Fill in the gaps with words from Ex. 3, then match the sentences with the types of stories/films mentioned in the list.**

thriller/horror, love story, detective story/mystery, action/adventure, science fiction

1 The chase scenes were so .... that I was on the edge of my seat.
2 It was such a(n) .... story, and the ending, when the lovers part forever, is very tragic.
3 There were some really .... monsters, and there was so much blood that I found it quite ....
4 The aliens were so .... that I almost believed they were real.
5 The plot was quite .... because the policemen had so many clues to follow up.

5 **Read the following book review and put the paragraphs in the correct order.**

Jane Eyre

A ☐ *The book is beautifully written, with poetic descriptions and excellent dialogue. The writer has created a dramatic, gripping plot with well-developed, very believable characters, letting us see into the soul of a sensitive but strong young woman.*

B ☐ *This book's fascinating plot is guaranteed to keep the reader absorbed from beginning to end. Don't miss your chance to read this classic masterpiece. Once you have read it, you will never forget it.*

C ☐ *Jane Eyre, the main character of the novel, is an orphan who has a very unhappy childhood. Despite this, she becomes a strong-willed young woman. When she leaves the orphanage she becomes the governess at Thornfield Hall, Mr Rochester's mansion. Strange things begin to happen there, and when a mysterious secret is revealed, Jane's life is changed forever.*

D ☐ *If you are looking for a romantic but mysterious story about a lonely woman who, after many strange experiences, finds lasting love, you should definitely read Jane Eyre by Charlotte Brontë.*

6 **Fill in the correct adjectives from the list below.**

dull, tragic, unbelievable, predictable, frightening, well-developed, original, shocking, highly entertaining, gripping

1 The story is extremely .... – I've never read anything like it before.
2 The characters were totally .... – no one would act like that in such a dangerous situation.
3 It is an absolutely .... film – I didn't take my eyes off the screen for a single instant.
4 The plot was so .... that you knew how the story was going to end from the first scene.
5 This .... play will keep you laughing from beginning to end.
6 The characters are so .... that by the end of the book you feel you've known them all your life.
7 There is a(n) .... scene near the end of the film in which the hero's wife dies in his arms.
8 Parts of the film were so .... that I nearly jumped out of my seat.
9 It's an extremely .... film – I would never let my children see it.
10 The characters were so .... that I wasn't at all interested in what happened to them.

7 **Write a review of a film/book you have seen or read recently.**

Study Check 3

A Describe a journey on which you met a particularly unpleasant person.

1 What kind of composition is this?
2 Which paragraph plan would you follow?
3 Which tenses would you use?
4 Does this topic require narrative and descriptive techniques?
5 Which techniques would you use to begin and end your composition?

B Last week you attended your best friend's wedding. Write a letter to your cousin describing the wedding and some of the people who were present.

1 What kind of letter is this?
2 Does this topic contain more than one aspect? If yes, which aspects does it contain?
3 Which techniques would you use to describe the atmosphere?
4 How would the use of adjectives and adverbs add to your description?
5 Would it be necessary to refer to the hobbies and interests of those present at the wedding? Why/Why not?

C You have seen the advertisement below. Write an email applying for the job.

Saving for your studies?
Don't know what to do this summer?
We've got the answer to your problems at
Sunfun Holiday Camp!
We're looking for young people to help run our holiday camp. There are all kinds of jobs available, from cooking to entertaining campers.
If you don't mind hard work contact:
SunfunHolidayCamp@hotmail.com

1 Should your email be formal or less formal?
2 Which paragraph plan would you follow?
3 Would you need to refer extensively to experience or qualifications in your email?
4 Which useful expressions would you use to begin and end your email?

D Your cousin wants to know about the scuba-diving course you went on last summer. You have kept the brochure and have made some notes on it. Looking at your notes, write a letter to your cousin giving him/her all the necessary information.

Crystal Bay Diving School

Discover this fantastic sport in the safe and beautiful surroundings of Crystal Bay!

- Full accommodation — only two meals provided
- Friendly instructors
- Practice pool — too shallow to practise in
- Modern equipment — some was old
- Daily boat trips out to areas full of sealife — only twice

1 What kind of letter would you write?
2 Is it necessary to cover all the points mentioned in the rubric?
3 What should you bear in mind when writing a transactional letter?
4 Suggest ways to begin and end your letter.

E "I woke up and started to scream. The room was full of smoke." Continue the story, describing how you escaped from the building.

1 Is it necessary to decide on a plot line before writing your story?
2 To make the order of events clear in your story, you should use: a) numbers, b) time words or c) sub-headings.
3 Which tense(s) would you use to: a) give the background of the story, b) set the scene and c) narrate events in sequence?
4 Which techniques would you use to begin and end your story?

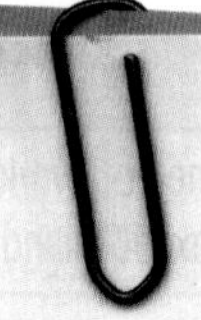

M Read the following topics and answer the questions:
- What type of article is each one?
- What style should be used in each?
- What information should be included in each article?
- What paragraph plan should be followed for each topic?

1 A health magazine is investigating the question: *Should smoking be banned in public places?* Write a short **article** for the magazine on this topic, based on your own experience.

2 An environmental magazine is investigating the question: *What can people do to help protect the environment?* Write a short **article** for the magazine on this topic, based on your own ideas and experience.

3 A computer magazine is investigating the question: *Should children be allowed to use computers?* Write a short **article** for the magazine.

4 Your college magazine has invited its readers to suggest ways of remembering new vocabulary in English. Write an **article** for the magazine, giving your suggestions.

5 An international young people's magazine is investigating the question: *Do young people today use their free time wisely?* Write a short **article** for the magazine on this topic based on your own experience.

6 An educational magazine has invited students to submit an article explaining why they started learning English. Write an **article** for the magazine.

7 A young people's magazine has asked its readers to submit descriptions of their favourite family member, commenting on how this person has influenced them. Write your **article** for the magazine.

Reports are normally formal pieces of writing and can be about assessing good and bad points, making proposals/ suggestions about something, or offering solutions to a problem. An appropriate heading and sub-headings should be included to make your points clear to the reader.

N Read the following topics and answer the questions:
- What type of report is each one?
- Who is the writer of each report? (e.g. employee, student, etc.)
- Who is each report written for?
- What information should be included in each?
- What would the main heading be for each report?
- What sub-headings can be used for each?

1 You work for a tourist agency and were recently asked to visit a new hotel in your area. You must now write a **report** for your boss, describing the hotel and what it offers holiday-makers. The report should include comments on its good and bad points.

2 Your pen-friend is doing a project on young people's TV viewing preferences, and has asked you to send him a report on the subject. Write the **report** for your pen-friend, explaining the TV viewing preferences of young people in your country.

3 You belong to a sports club which has recently received a large donation. The club is in need of new equipment. You have been asked to write a **report** on the club's facilities, suggesting ways to spend the money.

4 You are attending a summer language course and have been asked to write a report on a local leisure centre which the students have been using. Write your **report** describing the centre and what it offers, commenting on its good and bad points.

5 A local newspaper has invited its readers to write a report on a visit to a local department store. Write your **report** commenting on the shop's variety of products, service and prices. You can also mention any negative aspects.

6 You are working for your local tourist information office. You have been asked to write a report on shopping facilities in the area. The report will be used in a leaflet for people visiting your town. Write your **report.**

7 You work in a bookshop. The manager wants to make the shop more popular with young people and has asked you to write a report making some recommendations.
Write a **report** for your manager.

0 Read the following topics and answer these questions:
- What type of letter is required?
- What style should be used?
- How should you begin?
- How should you end?
- How should you address the recipient?
- How should you sign off?
- What information should you include?
- What paragraph plan should you follow?

1 You have just read this advertisement:

Wanted

Enthusiastic young people interested in becoming tour guides in their own areas. Applicants must have a good knowledge of French and German and an interest in local culture and history.

Write to: George Ditton, AMBITOURS, P.O. Box 397, Leeds

Write your **letter of application** to Ambitours in **120-180** words. Do not write any addresses.

2 Your friend has recently moved house and she feels very lonely in the new place. Write her a **letter** giving her advice on what to do to feel less lonely. Do not write any addresses.

3 You are taking part in an exchange programme. You will spend two weeks staying in the house of a French student living in Marseilles. Write a **letter** to the French student describing yourself and asking for details about his family and the town he lives in. Do not write any addresses.

4 This is part of an email you received from your English pen-friend, who has started attending a course studying your language in his/her country.

The course is fantastic and my teachers are well-qualified. Can you please suggest any ways of improving my understanding of the language? That would help me a lot.

Write your **email**, giving details of any activities, books, magazines, etc. you think might be useful, explaining how he/she could use them.

5 You are the president of your school's environmental action group and you have written to ask Mark Lewis, an environmentalist, to speak to your group. You have received the following reply:

I would be happy to speak to your students about my work with environmental protection groups. As I am travelling to Brazil at the end of the month, it would be best if we could arrange a date in the next two weeks. If you could give me two possible dates, I will let you know which suits me best.

Could you also tell me what exactly your students want to know, and what I should bring with me for the presentation?

Yours sincerely,
Mark Lewis

Read Mr Lewis's reply and the notes which you have made for yourself, then write a letter to him setting a date for the presentation and answering his other questions.

Notes
- general description of his work
- how he became involved
- slides showing environmental damage
- membership forms for students

Write a **letter** of **120 - 180** words. Do not write any addresses.

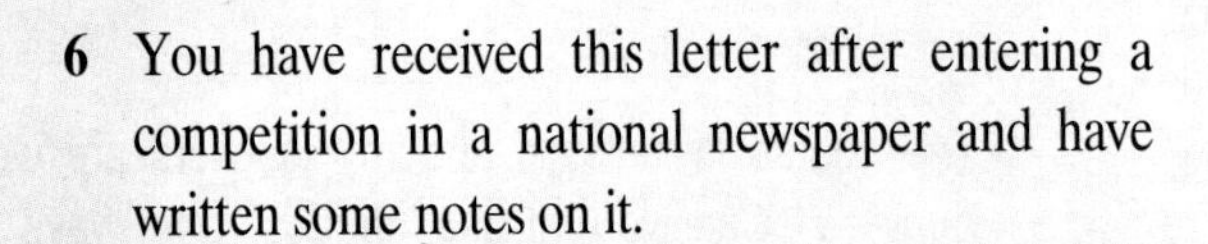

6 You have received this letter after entering a competition in a national newspaper and have written some notes on it.

The Daily Sentinel is delighted to announce that you are the winner in our Free Weekend in London competition.

You prize consists of:

- Free flights to and from London for two people ← exact date and times?
- Free accommodation at the Grand Hotel ← location?
- Tickets to a play at the Garrick Theatre ← what play?
- Evening meal at the Ritz ← which day- Saturday/ Sunday?
- Discount vouchers for seveal major London stores ← what kind of shops?

We would be grateful if you could let us know in advance of any special arrangements which need to be made, and would be happy to answer any queries you might have concerning the weekend. ← Yes

We look forward to hearing from you soon.

Yours sincerely,
Roger Britton

Read the letter along with your notes, then write your letter to the competition organiser including all your questions and requests. Write a **letter** of between **120** and **180** words in an appropriate style. Do not write any addresses.

P Read the topics below and comment on the following questions:
kind of writing? purpose of writing? content? target reader? style?

1 You participated in a project to help clean up a nearby beach, organised by a local newspaper. Those who participated had to write an article describing what the problems were and what they did to help solve them. Write your **article** for the newspaper.

2 You have been asked to contribute to a guidebook to be used by young visitors to your area. Write an **article** describing what sights and facilities would be most attractive to teenaged visitors.

3 A local radio station is running a "Best Parent of the Year" competition. To enter the competition you must write a short **composition** describing one of your parents.

4 An international young people's magazine is investigating the question:
Do today's young people show enough respect towards older people?
Write your **article** for the magazine.

5 An international magazine is asking for reports on television in various countries. Write your **report,** commenting on the variety and quality of TV programmes in your country.

6 Your school magazine has asked its readers to describe how their town has changed over the last thirty years. Write your **article**, describing the place and explaining whether these changes are for the better or for the worse.

7 A travel agency has asked its customers to write a description of their ideal holiday resort. The best description will win a one-week holiday for two at a destination of the winner's choice, all expenses paid. Write your **description** for the competition.

8 Your teacher has asked you to write a composition describing two of your family's most important possessions and explaining why they are important to you. Write your **composition.**

9 An international magazine is investigating the question:
Does violence in films and on TV increase violence in our everyday lives?
Write an **article**, giving your opinion on this subjec

10 You recently started working in a language school where you help to organise trips for students. Your boss has asked you to write a report on a museum in your area. Write your **report**, describing the museum, what it has to offer to students and commenting on its good and bad points.

11 Your teacher has asked your group to write compositions giving opinions and suggestions in answer to the following question:
"Is it harmful for students to have part-time jobs?
Write your **composition.**

12 You are a policeman. The chief police officer in the police station you work at has asked you to write a report suggesting ways to reduce crime in your area. Write your **report** commenting on the area's crime rate and what you feel should be done to reduce it.

13 The company you work for has asked you to write a report suggesting ways to improve working conditions in the company. Write your **report**, commenting on the working conditions and how these can be improved.

14 Your teacher has asked you to write about a photograph from your family album which is very important to you. Write a **composition** describing what the picture shows and what memories it brings back to you, explaining the reasons why this picture is important to you.

15 You accidentally left your briefcase, which contained some important documents, on a train. Write a **letter** of **120-180** words to the lost property officer enquiring about your briefcase. Do not write any addresses.

16 Your teacher has asked you to write a story for the school magazine. The story must begin with the following words:
Sally read through the letter once more before throwing it onto the fire. Now she knew what she had to do.

17 You have been invited to a reception organised by your company in order to introduce the new Managing Director but you will be unable to attend because you will be at a conference. Write a **letter** explaining why you will not be able to attend the reception. Do not write any addresses.

18 A local magazine is running a short story competition. To enter the competition you have to submit a story which must begin with the following words:
I sighed with relief as I sat back in the compartment of the first class carriage. "They would never catch me now," I thought.

19 An international young people's magazine is investigating the question:
Would one international language unite or divide us?
Write a short **article** for the magazine on this topic.

20 You read this advertisement in this week's *Daily Issues* but you need more information. Read carefully the advertisement and the notes which you have made. Then, write a letter to the Childhelp Centre, covering the points in your notes. Write a **letter** of between **120** and **180** words in an appropriate style. Do not write any addresses.

CHILDHELP
We are looking for young volunteers to organise and supervise activities for children with physical disabilities. If you are sportsminded, artistic or have any special skills which you would like to share with children who have mobility problems, we are looking for you. Flexible hours.
Write to: Marie Starkey, Childhelp Centre, POBox 236 Severton, Hants

age limit?
wood working/ gardening
OK evenings?
near town centre?

INTERPRETING RUBRICS

When you read the rubric for a writing task, you should always pay careful attention to the key words and phrases. These will help you to decide on:

- **Type of writing** – look for words which tell you about the format and layout expected, such as *Report, Letter, Article, Composition,* etc.
- **Reason for writing** – when you read the rubric, your reason for writing should be clear. Look for key words/phrases such as *suggesting, giving your opinion, to explain, to apply for the job, to persuade, to describe,* etc.
- **Situation and target reader** – phrases such as *your school, your friend, your teacher,* etc, help you to decide what you should write and who will read it.
- **Style of writing** – this depends on the target reader, e.g. you should use *formal writing* if you are writing a report for your superior, *less formal* writing if you are writing an article for your school magazine, *informal* if you are writing a letter to a friend of yours.
- **Subjects/Topics to include** – key words/phrases indicate the main subjects of your piece of writing, e.g. *a letter asking for information, a report suggesting places to visit,* etc. The rubric can help you with the paragraph plan. For example, if the rubric says: *Write a letter in which you include details of your qualifications, experience and the reasons why you want the job,* you could write one paragraph each about qualifications, experience and reasons.

In some writing tasks, you have to respond to prompt material, e.g. *a letter which you have received, an article you have read,* etc. In these cases, it is important to include all of the relevant points, rephrased in your own words.

1 Read the rubric, underline the key words and answer the questions.

You are planning a surprise party for one of your friends who is leaving the area and have written to your best friend, Tim, to ask him to help you with the organisation. Read Tim's letter and the notes you have made. Then, using this information, write back to Tim and tell him whether or not you agree with his suggestions. Write your letter. You should write between 120 and 180 words.

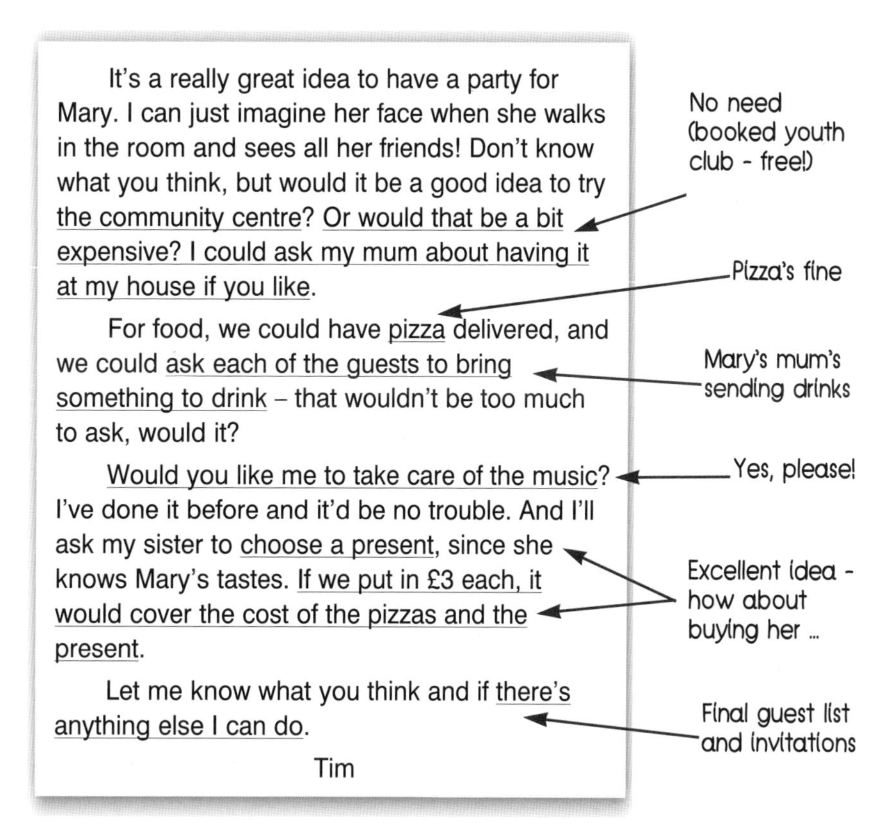

It's a really great idea to have a party for Mary. I can just imagine her face when she walks in the room and sees all her friends! Don't know what you think, but would it be a good idea to try the community centre? Or would that be a bit expensive? I could ask my mum about having it at my house if you like.

For food, we could have pizza delivered, and we could ask each of the guests to bring something to drink – that wouldn't be too much to ask, would it?

Would you like me to take care of the music? I've done it before and it'd be no trouble. And I'll ask my sister to choose a present, since she knows Mary's tastes. If we put in £3 each, it would cover the cost of the pizzas and the present.

Let me know what you think and if there's anything else I can do.

Tim

1 What type of writing should you use?
2 What is your reason for writing?
3 Who is the target reader? What style is appropriate?
4 How many points must you include? Suggest how you could rephrase them.
5 How will you arrange these points into paragraphs?
6 What information should you include in your opening paragraph?
7 How will you end your letter?

2 a) **Read models A and B below, and say which one is more suitable. Consider:**

- paragraphing
- style
- inclusion of relevant points
- rephrasing
- addressing the reader

Dear Tim,

1 Thanks for getting back to me about Mary's party. I'm glad you think it's a good idea and can help me out.

2 Firstly, about the venue. I've already booked the youth club and they've said we don't need to pay because Mary is a member!

3 As for the food, I think ordering pizza is a brilliant idea, and we don't need to worry about the drinks because Mary's mum is going to send some to the youth club for us.

4 As far as the music is concerned, it would be fantastic if you could take care of it. And I think it's a great idea to ask Julie to get Mary's present. What about some CDs? I think if we put in £3 each that should be quite enough.

5 The only thing that is left to do is to write out a guest list and send out the invitations. Do you think you'd be able to do that for me since you know everyone?

6 I think that's everything. Thanks again - see you on the 18th!

Love,
Lisa

B

My dear friend,

1 I would like to express my gratitude for your prompt reply. I am writing to let you know what we should do for Mary's party. Pizza's fine and Mary's mum is sending drinks.

2 It would be a good idea to use the community centre but there's no need (booked youth club – free!). You asked if you should take care of the music. Yes, please!

3 It's an excellent idea for your sister to choose a present for her. How about buying her a watch. £3 each should cover the cost of the pizzas and the watch.

4 Did you see the match on Saturday? What a fantastic goal! I have it on video if you missed it and I'll bring it to the party if you want. See you at the party.

Kind regards,
Steve

b) **Now read the *good* model again and answer the questions.**

1 What style has the letter been written in? Why has this style been used?
2 Suggest a suitable alternative first paragraph.
3 How has the writer begun each of the main body paragraphs? How could you begin each paragraph differently?
4 How have the notes from the rubric been rephrased?
5 Suggest a suitable alternative final paragraph.

Introduction

Paragraph 1

reason for writing / opening remarks

Main Body

Paragraphs 2-4

expanded, paraphrased notes from the letter

Paragraph 5

request for help with guest list and invitations

Conclusion

Final Paragraph

closing remarks

3 Read the rubric, underline the key words and answer the questions.

You are going to take part in an exchange programme which will involve you staying with an English family for a month in the summer. You receive an email from the family you will be staying with, part of which is printed below. Read the email and the notes you have made on it. Then write a suitable reply to Mr Graham, in which you cover all the points in your notes. Write your email. You should write between 120 and 180 words.

New Message

From: David Graham
Sent: 25 April
Subject: exchange programme

We are very much looking forward to your stay with us and I thought I would write and clear up one or two details.

Firstly, I understand that you will be arriving on June 30th and will stay until July 15th. Is this still the arrangement?

There are two spare rooms and you can choose which one you'd prefer. The larger room is downstairs and has a door into the garden. There is also a smaller room in the attic which has a telephone socket and a window overlooking the river.

Also, my wife would like to know if you are a vegetarian or if there is any food that you don't eat. If there is anything else we can do to make your stay more comfortable, don't hesitate to let us know.

We'll all be there to meet you at the airport, so could you let us know the details as soon as you have them.

Looking forward to seeing you,

David Graham

1 What style of writing should you use? Why?
2 How would you organise your writing into paragraphs?
3 Which of the following sentences would be suitable for your email? Give reasons.

a ☐ Unfortunately, there has been a change in the dates.
b ☐ I'm staying until the 28th and there's nothing I can do about it.
c ☐ I don't care which room I have – it's all the same to me.
d ☐ I don't mind which room I have – I'm sure either will be fine.
e ☐ I'm not a vegetarian but I'm not very fond of fish.
f ☐ I can't eat fish because it makes me sick.
g ☐ I need a computer and a TV in my room.
h ☐ Is there a computer that I could use for a few hours a week?

4 How could you start/end your email?

4 a) **Read model A and, in pairs, underline the irrelevant information. Say what information from the notes the writer has included.**

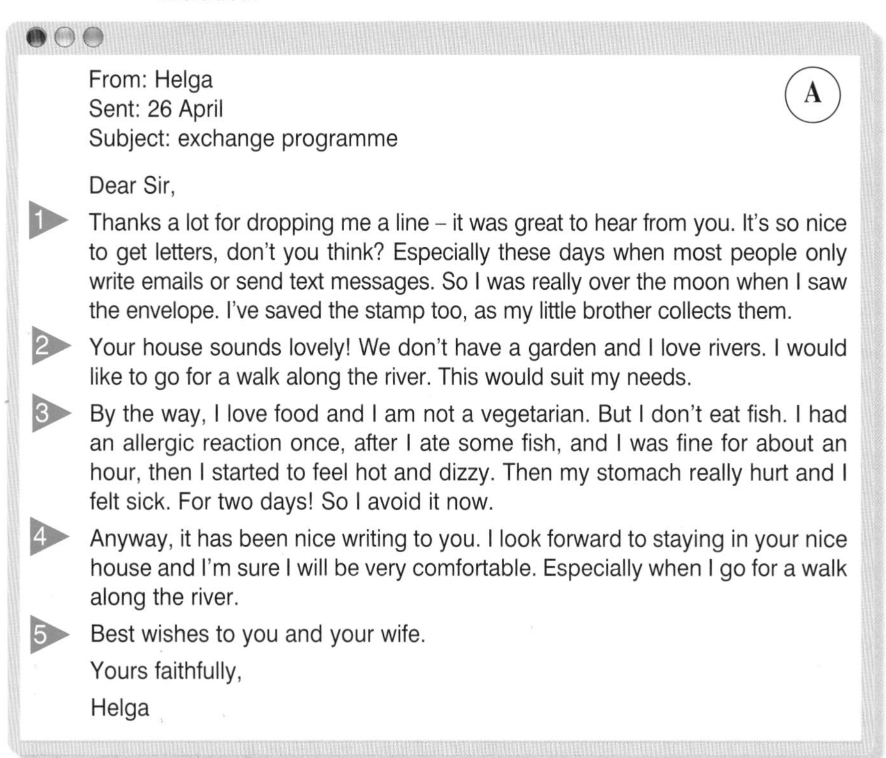

From: Helga
Sent: 26 April
Subject: exchange programme

A

Dear Sir,

1 Thanks a lot for dropping me a line – it was great to hear from you. It's so nice to get letters, don't you think? Especially these days when most people only write emails or send text messages. So I was really over the moon when I saw the envelope. I've saved the stamp too, as my little brother collects them.

2 Your house sounds lovely! We don't have a garden and I love rivers. I would like to go for a walk along the river. This would suit my needs.

3 By the way, I love food and I am not a vegetarian. But I don't eat fish. I had an allergic reaction once, after I ate some fish, and I was fine for about an hour, then I started to feel hot and dizzy. Then my stomach really hurt and I felt sick. For two days! So I avoid it now.

4 Anyway, it has been nice writing to you. I look forward to staying in your nice house and I'm sure I will be very comfortable. Especially when I go for a walk along the river.

5 Best wishes to you and your wife.

Yours faithfully,

Helga

b) **Read model B and, in pairs, find the points from the notes. Has the writer included all of them? How have they been rephrased?**

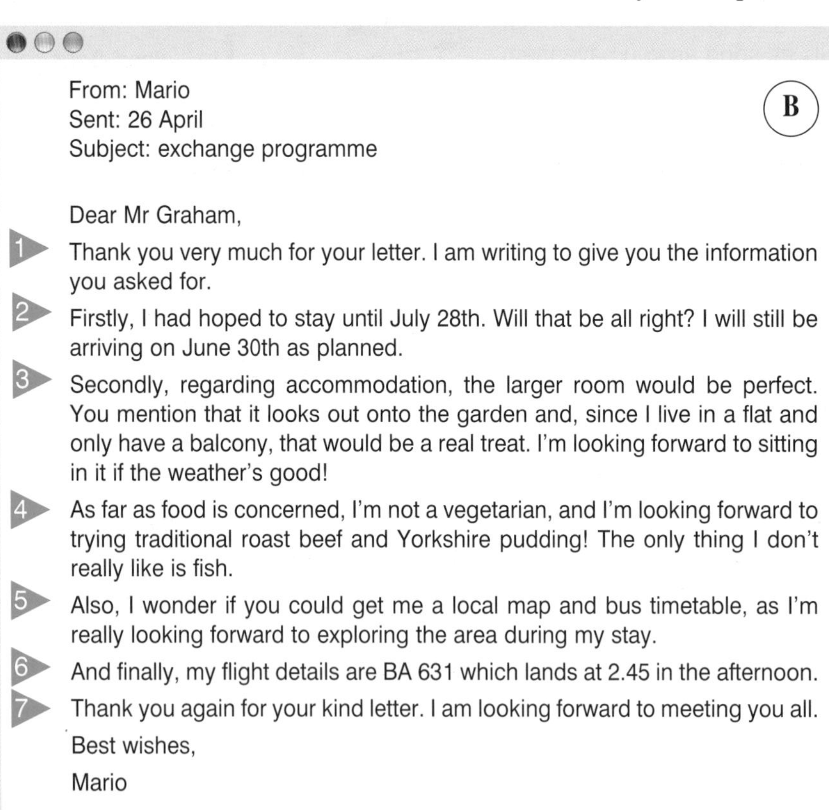

From: Mario
Sent: 26 April
Subject: exchange programme

B

Dear Mr Graham,

1 Thank you very much for your letter. I am writing to give you the information you asked for.

2 Firstly, I had hoped to stay until July 28th. Will that be all right? I will still be arriving on June 30th as planned.

3 Secondly, regarding accommodation, the larger room would be perfect. You mention that it looks out onto the garden and, since I live in a flat and only have a balcony, that would be a real treat. I'm looking forward to sitting in it if the weather's good!

4 As far as food is concerned, I'm not a vegetarian, and I'm looking forward to trying traditional roast beef and Yorkshire pudding! The only thing I don't really like is fish.

5 Also, I wonder if you could get me a local map and bus timetable, as I'm really looking forward to exploring the area during my stay.

6 And finally, my flight details are BA 631 which lands at 2.45 in the afternoon.

7 Thank you again for your kind letter. I am looking forward to meeting you all.

Best wishes,

Mario

c) **Now read model B again and answer the questions.**

1 What do you think Mr Graham's reaction to the email will be? Give reasons. Think about: register, style, content.
2 How could the paragraphs be organised differently?
3 What else could you mention in paragraph 5?

Introduction

Paragraph 1

reason for writing / opening remarks

Main Body

Paragraphs 2-6

expanded, paraphrased notes from the letter

Conclusion

Final Paragraph

closing remarks

5 Read the rubric, underline the key words and say what information you must include in your letter.

You are going on a four-day excursion to England with your English class and have received the programme of events below from the director of your college, Mr Dawson.

After a discussion, however, the members of your class have decided that they would very much like to go to a film festival which they have seen in an advertisement. They have asked you to write to the director. Read the programme, the advertisement and your notes, and then use this information to write a **letter** to Mr Dawson. You should write between 120 and 180 words.

England Trip, June 2004
Programme of events:

Monday 5th
London sightseeing tour
Visit to Art Gallery

Tuesday 6th
Day Trip to Oxford

Wednesday 7th
Study Day (everyone must attend! – see separate programme)

Thursday 8th
Free day for Souvenir Shopping
Airport transfer 23.00

5th – 9th June Jubilee Hall, London

2nd Annual British Film Festival
For the second year running, we will be showing the very best of British cinema.
Come and see some of the great masterpieces – and not a Hollywood movie in sight!

Films shown from 10.00 – 22.00

Special discount for group bookings!

Notes for letter to Mr Dawson

- Great programme, especially ...
- Mention film festival
- Fantastic opportunity (say why)
- Suggest going instead of ... (decide!)
- Mention booking

6 a) Read models A and B, and say which one is written in an inappropriate style. Give examples.

A

Dear Mr Dawson,

1 I am writing with regard to the programme of events for the forthcoming trip to England.

2 We are very happy with the choice of events, in particular the sightseeing tour of London, and are looking forward to the day trip to Oxford. In addition, we would also very much like to attend a British film festival that is taking place in London during our visit. I think it is a good idea, as it will be an excellent opportunity to practise our English and to see films which might not be available at home.

3 If you agree, it will be necessary to change the programme slightly. I suggest we attend the film festival in the afternoon of the Monday instead of visiting the art gallery. I have spoken to everyone who is going on the trip and they all agree to this. We will have to book in advance, as the festival is very popular. However, if we book as a group, we will get a reduced price.

4 I hope you will accept my suggestion and I look forward to receiving your answer as soon as possible.

Yours sincerely,

Kathy Kendal

B

Dear Mr Dawson,

1 I am in receipt of the programme of events for our forthcoming trip to London. My fellow students have asked me to write to you, however, to request a minor alteration to the proposed schedule.

2 The programme looks really cool, especially the tour of London and the visit to the art gallery. We're all looking forward to it.

3 Nevertheless, please note that the 2nd Annual British Film Festival is on from the 5th to the 9th of June at the Jubilee hall. It would be a fantastic opportunity for us to attend, as most of us will not be able to return to England for some time. The films are all in English so it will be educational and there'll be none of that Hollywood rubbish so you needn't worry!

4 Perhaps we could go there on Tuesday 6th instead of the trip to Oxford. I hope you will not be unduly inconvenienced by my suggestion and that it will meet with your approval.

5 Well, it's up to you in the end. You're the boss so you will have the last word. Keep me informed on the matter. I look forward to hearing from you in due course.

Yours truly,

Helena

b) Now read the *good* model again and answer the questions.

1 How does the writer rephrase the note, "*Great programme – especially ...*"?

2 What reasons does the writer give for attending the film festival?

3 Which event does the writer suggest dropping in favour of the film festival? How is this decision justified?

4 Underline the topic sentences. Then, in pairs, suggest other appropriate ones.

5 Do you think Mr Dawson will agree to the suggestion after reading this letter? Why (not)?

Introduction

Paragraph 1

reason for writing

Main Body

Paragraphs 2-3

expanded, paraphrased notes

Conclusion

Final Paragraph

closing remarks

7 Read the rubric, underline the key words and answer the questions.

You have been doing a project on communication as part of your English course. Now your teacher has asked you to write a composition about the following statement:
The use of computer technology will totally change the way we communicate in the future.
Write your **composition**. You should write between 120 and 180 words.

1 What type of composition is this?
2 How formal does your writing need to be? Why?
3 Say whether the following statements are true or false:

a You could write a composition about the invention of the computer. ....
b You must include the disadvantages of computers. ....
c Your composition should focus on what you think will happen in the future. ....
d What you write should be mostly about communication. ....
e You could mention e-mails, text messages and fax machines. ....
f You should divide your writing clearly into paragraphs. ....

8 a) Read model A and find references to the future. Then find words and phrases in the model that mean the same as the following:

the usual way, it will not be long, costs less, most people would agree, I predict will continue, firstly, am convinced

A

1 No one can deny that computers have made communicating far easier and much faster. This is a trend that I see continuing in the future.

2 To begin with, the Internet allows people from all over the world to chat to one another on line. Furthermore, using email or sending text messages takes less time than letter writing and it is cheaper than making phone calls. It is difficult to now imagine that we will ever go back to the old-fashioned ways of keeping in contact with people.

3 In addition, computer technology is responsible for all of the latest developments in communications. More and more people are using mobile phones to stay in touch, either in the conventional way or by sending text messages. As further progress is made, these devices will become more sophisticated. We already have mobile phones with email capability. It is only a matter of time before we are all using electronic means to communicate.

4 All in all, I think that computer technology has revolutionised the way people communicate. Progress in this area is very rapid. I believe that we will see even more developments in the future.

Introduction

Paragraph 1

clearly stated topic and opinion

Main Body

Paragraphs 2-3

viewpoints and reasons

Conclusion

Final Paragraph

restated opinion, prediction for the future

b) Underline the topic sentences in the main body paragraphs. In pairs, think of other appropriate ones.

c) Circle all the linkers which the writer uses to list points; to add points; to conclude. Then, replace them with other appropriate ones.

d) In pairs, think of another paragraph to conclude the composition.

e) Now read model B and say which paragraph:

.... does not focus enough on the future.
.... contains three words used wrongly. Correct them.
.... is very repetitive. Give examples.
.... is too informal in style. Give examples.
.... talks about computers but not about communication.
.... should be separated into two paragraphs.
.... is badly punctuated. Correct it.

B

1 The way we communicate now is rapidly changing because of the widespread use of computers. It is now possible to communicate very rapidly and we can look forward to a time when everybody on the planet can communicate with everybody else because of the even more widespread use of computers.

2 The traditional way of communicating, writing letters by hand, was much more personal because the writer had time to refine and think out the contents of the letter before sending it and many people still prefer this method even though it is a lot slower.

3 Furthermore, computers are extremely useful in education. Classrooms which give students access to computers are increasingly common and there is little doubt that this will benefit young learners. Computer technology is also widely used in industry. We should not forget that many of the appliances and vehicles that we have today are assembled by robots which, in turn, are controlled by computers. As this technology progresses, we are likely to see major new developments.

4 Well, it looks like computers are going to continue to effect the way we communicate, either we like it or not! There's no much point in complaining – we might as well just get used to it.

9 **a) Read the rubric, underline the key words and answer the questions.**

> You have recently had a class discussion about education. Now your English teacher has asked you to write a composition in which you give your opinions on the following statement:
>
> *School is no longer useful or necessary.*
>
> Write your **composition**. You should write between 120 and 180 words.

1 What type of writing is this?
2 Who is the target reader? What style is appropriate? Why?
3 What is your reason for writing?
4 What should you include? List them in paragraphs.
5 Fill in the table below with ideas of your own.

Good points about school	Bad points about school
....	....
....	....
....	....
....	....

b) Now say whether you would agree or disagree with the statement in the rubric.

10 **Read the model and answer the questions.**

1 *In my opinion*, going to school is an important part of growing up. For this reason I would say that school is both useful and necessary.

2 *First of all*, children get an education there, as well as learning important social skills, such as how to relate to others and be part of a team. It also teaches them discipline, the importance of following rules and a respect for authority. Apart from that, school is an excellent place to make friends.

3 *However*, it cannot be denied that in some cases schools do not teach children the skills required to live and work in the real world. Critics often claim that some of the subjects taught are no longer relevant. Nevertheless, I still believe that the advantages outweigh the disadvantages.

4 *In conclusion*, I think that, overall, school is beneficial to children. It would be better to change teaching methods rather than close schools altogether, because if that were to happen, a lot of children would be missing out on an important part of childhood.

1 Is the writer *in favour of* or *against* the statement in the rubric? Where does he/she say so?
2 Where does the writer mention the opposing viewpoint? Why is this included?
3 Suggest alternatives for the words and phrases in italics.
4 Underline the topic sentences. Then in pairs suggest other appropriate ones.

Introduction

Paragraph 1

clearly stated topic and opinion

Main Body

Paragraph 2

viewpoints and reasons

Paragraph 3

opposing viewpoint and reason(s)

Conclusion

Final Paragraph

restated paraphrased opinion

11 **Read the rubric, underline the key words and answer the questions on the right.**

Your school has been asked to make suggestions for a documentary that is going to be made about the area where you live. Your teacher has asked you to write a report in which you suggest the places and activities that should be filmed, giving reasons why they should be included in the documentary.
Write your **report**. You should write between 120 and 180 words.

1 Who is the target reader? What style of writing is appropriate?
2 Which of the following would be suitable for inclusion in your report?
A street market ☐
Your classroom ☐ A park ☐
The sea front ☐
A shopping centre ☐
Other ....
3 For each of the points you have ticked above, give reasons for your answers.

12 **Read the model and answer the questions.**

To: Mrs Barrett
From: Lea Thompson
Subject: TV documentary
Date: 31st January 2...

Introduction
The aim of this report is to suggest places and activities of local interest to be included in the proposed Channel 5 documentary on Whitecliff.

Blue Cove Marina
Apart from the picturesque harbour, there are antique shops, boutiques, and a lively, bustling atmosphere. The marina's inclusion in the documentary would be a good way to portray some of the more traditional aspects of the town.

Arndale Shopping Centre
This modern shopping complex has all the well-known high street stores, plus a mini funfair, a multi-screen cinema and several busy cafes. Including it in the documentary would show people that Whitecliff has something for all the family.

Melton Park
Promoting the park's many features would be an ideal way to show the things that people can do all year round. People could be filmed picnicking by the lake in summer, while in winter, scenes could be shot of children making snowmen beside the frozen pond.

Conclusion
I feel that the places I have selected will show Whitecliff at its best. By featuring these different activities, viewers would get the chance to see the variety that the town has to offer.

1 How does the report begin? How does it differ from a letter?
2 How is the model divided into paragraphs?
3 Circle the descriptive adjectives which have been used.
4 For each of the main body sections, say what reasons have been given.
5 How does the writer end the report?

Introduction

Paragraph 1
purpose of report

Main Body

Paragraphs 2-4
places and reasons (in separate sections with headings)

Conclusion

Final Paragraph
summary of recommendations

13 Read the rubric, underline the key words and answer the questions.

A book is going to be published containing interesting places for visitors to your area. The publishing company you are working for has been contacted for suggestions about which places should be included. Now your manager has asked you to write a report describing one place and giving your reasons why you would recommend it to visitors.
Write your **report**. You should write between 120 and 180 words.

1 How formal does your writing need to be? Give reasons.
2 Which of the following section headings could you include in your report?
Things to See ☐ Conclusion ☐
Opening Times ☐
Recreation ☐ Introduction ☐
How to Get There ☐ Other ☐
3 Which words/phrases could you use to recommend the place?

14 Read the two models and say which is better, giving reasons. Think about:

- layout
- style
- appropriateness of subheadings
- well-justified reasons
- use of language
- grammar

(A)

To: Mr Garside
From: David Bennett
Subject: Glendalough
Date: 21st March 2...

1 **Introduction**
The purpose of this report is to suggest the inclusion of Glendalough in the forthcoming book of places that visitors may find of interest.

2 **Things to See**
Glendalough has a colourful history which visitors can discover while admiring some of the most fantastic scenery in Ireland. Remains include a complete Norman round tower and other stone buildings from about 600 AD, all among freshwater lakes and granite mountains.

3 **Recreation**
There is a great deal to do here. Fishing is a popular activity at the lakes, while the more energetic can go hill walking. The area is also used by picnickers and the views are so breathtaking that it is ideal for anyone with an interest in photography.

4 **Conclusion**
Glendalough comes highly recommended for fresh air enthusiasts whether young or old, and is a great day out for all the family. For these reasons I feel it deserves a place in the book.

Introduction

Paragraph 1
purpose of report, name of place

Main Body

Paragraphs 2-3
description, different aspects of place (in separate sections with headings)

Conclusion

Final Paragraph
general comment / final recommendation

B

The Most Interesting Places

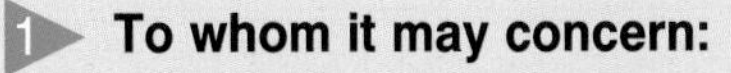

To whom it may concern:

I'm writing you this report is to make a suggestion of an interesting place to be included in a book for visitors to this area. I would suggest that Wexham Castle would be ideal for this purpose. It's hard, though, because there are so many nice places. The castle dates back to the time of The Crusades but has been added to and parts of it have been rebuilt several times between then and now and guided tours of the building occur three times per day.

Grounds

The castle is on a hillside within four acres of forested land. It is a very green area and there are animals.

Get Lost!

As you enter the castle, there is a nice garden and a very nice maze. The caretaker often has to guide visitors who cannot find their way out.

And Finally!

With its rich historical background and extensive grounds, Wexham Castle is an ideal place for people to visit and explore. I would strongly recommend that this site will be included in the book as a place of interest. Don't miss it – it's fun for all the family!

15 Read the rubric, underline the key words and answer the questions.

- You have seen the following in a magazine for learners of English.

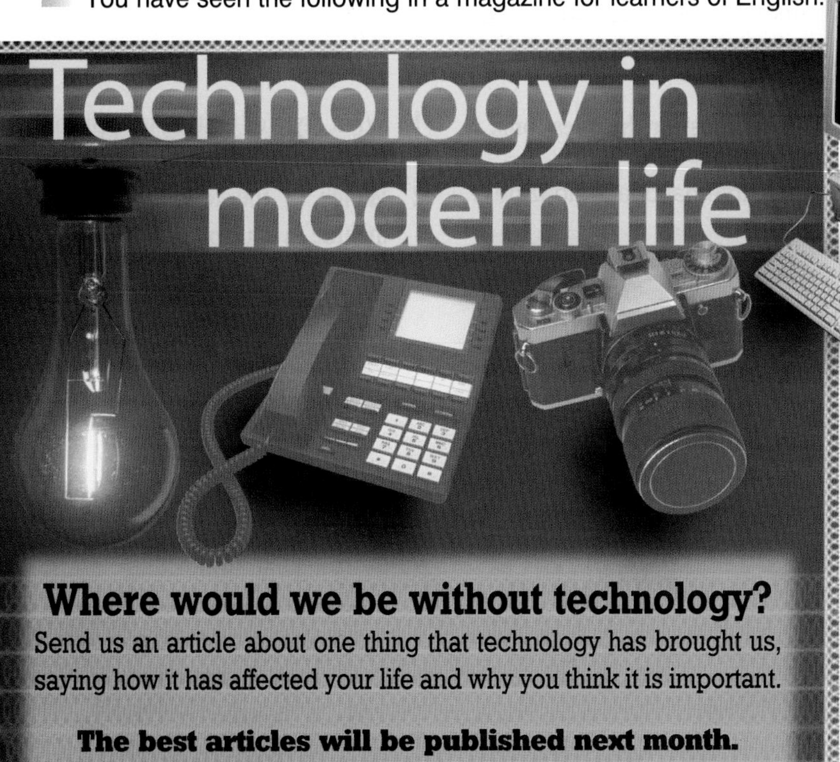

- Write your **article**. You should write between 120 and 180 words.

1 What type of writing is it?
2 Who is going to read it?
3 What style of writing should you use? Why?
4 How many items should you write about?
5 What two things must you mention?

16 Read the article and answer the questions.

Where would we be without technology?

1 Throughout the 20th century, technology provided us with a huge variety of new developments. In my opinion, one of the greatest gifts technology has given us is the telephone.

2 Firstly, phones have improved our relationships by helping us communicate quickly. I spend hours on the phone talking to my friends and family and it helps me stay in contact with those who live in different parts of the country and abroad. Sometimes you just don't have the energy to write a letter and it takes so long to get there, phoning is much more convenient and personal.

3 What's more, mobile phones are very useful in serious situations. Examples include following an accident, if your car breaks down in the middle of nowhere, or if you get stuck in a lift. I find mine most useful when I'm meeting a friend and one of us is going to be late or has got lost.

4 All in all, I think the telephone is one of the best inventions. It exists to make our lives easier and bring people closer together, and that can only be a good thing!

Introduction

Paragraph 1

clearly stated topic and your choice

Main Body

Paragraphs 2-3

viewpoints & justification examples

Conclusion

Final Paragraph

briefly restated opinion / final thoughts

1 What, according to the writer, are the main benefits of the telephone? In which paragraphs does he mention them? What examples does he mention?
2 Which linkers does the writer use to introduce each point? Suggest alternatives.
3 Underline the topic sentences. Then in pairs think of other supporting sentences.
4 What point does the writer make in the final paragraph? Which other paragraph contains the same point?
5 Suggest another ending.

17 Read the rubric, underline the key words and answer the questions.

You see the following announcement in an international magazine.

Every month, we invite the readers of this magazine to send in their own articles. This month:

The Transport of Tomorrow

How do you think we will be travelling around in, say, fifty years' time? Will we still be using cars? If so, what will they look like?
And what about public transport? Will it still be the same?

Interesting prizes for the best articles!

Have your say!

Write your **article**. You should write between 120 and 180 words.

1 What style of writing is appropriate for this article? Why?
2 Which of the following must you include in your piece of writing?
- Your views on the magazine ☐
- Your favourite form of transport ☐
- Your predictions about the use of cars in the future ☐
- Your predictions about the design of cars in the future ☐
- What you think about public transport today ☐
- How you think public transport will be different in the future ☐
- A reference to the prizes for the best articles ☐

18 **Read the model and answer the questions.**

The Transport of Tomorrow

1 It is very difficult to predict what kind of transport we will have in the future. I've no doubt that in fifty years we will still be travelling around in cars, and public transport will almost certainly exist. However, I think they will be very different to what we have today.

2 To begin with, technology is progressing so quickly that every year cars come on the market with new gadgetry. In several years they'll probably be so fast they'll break the sound barrier! I imagine they'll also be more compact and even standard models will have built-in navigation systems. These will probably be voice activated, so all the driver has to do is state his destination and the car will take him there.

3 As for public transport, it will probably be powered by electricity. For instance, electric trams are already in use in many cities and more are being introduced because they cause less pollution. There will also be vast electric underground systems that go on for miles beneath the city.

4 To sum up, I think in fifty years' time we'll be able to get to our destination more quickly, cheaply and comfortably – without damaging the environment.

Introduction

Paragraph 1

clearly stated topic / general opinion

Main Body

Paragraph 2

predictions about cars

Paragraph 3

predictions about public transport

Conclusion

Final Paragraph

restated opinion / closing comment

1 How does the writer begin the article? In pairs, think of another beginning.
2 What is the main subject of paragraph 2? How does the writer support his or her viewpoints?
3 What is the main subject of paragraph 3? What examples does the writer use?
4 How does the writer conclude the article? In pairs, think of another ending.

19 **Read the rubric, underline the key words and answer the questions.**

You have been asked by your English teacher to write a story for the college magazine. Your story must **begin** with the following words: *Although I didn't want to do it, I knew I had no choice.*
Write your **story**. You should write between 120 and 180 words.

1 What kind of things might you *not want to do*?
2 In what circumstances might you *not have any choice*?
3 Tick the elements below that you think make a good story:

A variety of descriptive language	☐
An interesting beginning	☐
A complicated plot	☐
Suspense	☐
Atmosphere	☐
A lot of different characters	☐
A satisfactory ending	☐

4 What tenses will you mostly use?
5 Think of time linkers you could use in your story.
6 Is it going to be a first person or third person narrative? Who is the main character?

20 a) **Read the two stories below and say which one is not suitable. What are the biggest problems with this story? Look for examples of the writer:**

- not following the instructions in the rubric
- using the wrong tense
- using the wrong word
- not using proper punctuation

A

1 I had to tell Tony. Although I didn't want to do it, I knew I really had no choice. Since our first meeting, at college, working voluntary at the Student Union office, we joined the work between us. Lately however Tony is making my life a misery. Suddenly he was coming to college late I was covering for him on missed deadlines, and then one day I decided that this must end.

2 I waited for him to arrive; I rose from my seat and stopped him just before he could reach the coffee pot. I told him angry that I had enough, either you do your share of the work or find another partner I shouted.

3 He did not say to me for the rest of the day. However, the next day I arrived to find Tony catching up on some of the work he abandoned. He only stopped long enough to apologise for the way he has been behaving lately. Since then, we have been the best of friends. We never spoke of the incident since.

B

1 Although I didn't want to do it, I knew I had no choice. I had been asked to give a speech in front of the whole school on the last day of term. My teacher had not listened to me when I had tried to get out of it. So for weeks, I prepared my speech, getting more and more anxious.

2 When the day came, I stood at the back of the stage, trying really hard to stay calm. I was shaking so badly that I couldn't see the words on the page. All of a sudden, my name was called.

3 As I walked nervously towards the front of the stage, I could see all my classmates grinning and whispering to each other. With my heart pounding, I glanced briefly at my notes, took a deep breath and started to speak. To my surprise, I soon began to feel more relaxed. By the time I reached the final page of my notes, I was actually starting to enjoy myself.

4 Once I had finished, I breathed a huge sigh of relief. Not only was it over, but it hadn't been nearly as bad as I had feared.

b) **Now read the *good* model again and answer the questions.**

1 Underline the information in the first paragraph that tells the reader:
   a who was involved
   b where the action took place
   c when the action took place
   d what the writer didn't want to do
2 Which words and phrases show the writer's feelings?
3 Find examples of different verb tenses. Why have these tenses been used?
4 Circle the time references in the story.
5 Underline the descriptive adjectives, adverbs and verbs. What difference do they make to the story?
6 In point form, list the events as they happened. Which is the climax event?

Introduction

Paragraph 1

(begin with the words given) set the scene (who - where - when - what)

Main Body

Paragraphs 2-3

develop the story - main events in the order they happened

Conclusion

Final Paragraph

end of story / feelings / comments

21 **Read the rubric, underline the key words and answer the questions.**

> You have decided to enter a short story competition that you saw in a magazine. The magazine stated that your story must **end** with the following words:
>
> *Exhausted, he closed his eyes and fell into a deep sleep.*
>
> Write your **story**. You should write between 120 and 180 words.

1 Is it a first or third person narrative?
2 Who is going to read your story?
3 What information could you include in the first paragraph?
4 When do people usually feel exhausted?
5 How will you end your story?

22 a) **Read the model and answer the questions.**

1 It was a winter's morning and James was walking his dog, Maisie, along the sea front. It was raining heavily and the waves were pounding against the harbour wall.

2 James threw a stick and it landed right on the edge. As Maisie rushed to fetch it, she fell with a loud splash into the sea. James ran along the harbour yelling frantically for help. He knew Maisie would drown if he didn't pull her out soon but he couldn't get close to her.

3 James was about to jump into the sea himself when, suddenly, he noticed a rope on the pavement. Reaching down, he grabbed the rope and, holding tightly to one end, threw it with all his strength into the sea. Immediately, the dog bit the rope so James was able to slowly pull her in.

4 By the time they got home, they were both soaked but glad to be safe. Later that day, sitting in his favourite armchair, with Maisie at his feet and the fire turned up high, James thought about their lucky escape. Exhausted, he closed his eyes and fell into a deep sleep.

Introduction

Paragraph 1

set the scene (who - where - when - what)

Main Body

Paragraphs 2-3

develop the story - main events in the order they happened

Conclusion

Final Paragraph

end of story / feelings / comments (end with words given)

1 How does the writer set the scene?
2 What was the first event in the story?
3 How do you (the reader) feel at the end of paragraph 2?
4 List the events of the story in point form.
5 Underline the phrases the writer uses to describe the weather.
6 What tenses have been used? Why?
7 Circle the linkers (and, but, so, etc) the writer uses to join sentences.
8 What is the climax event in the story?

b) **In pairs, think of your own story for the competition. List the events in point form, then use your list to tell your story to the class.**

23 **Read the rubric, underline the key words and answer the questions.**

You see this advertisement for a summer job.

Westford Festival

We need people of all ages to help in the preparation and running of this year's festival, due to take place in September.

Remember, we are not interested in exam grades or qualifications! We need energetic and cheerful people (who can speak *some* English) to:

- help in the planning of events, exhibitions, etc
- look after young children and organise activities for them
- do odd jobs like painting, delivering leaflets, putting up posters, etc

Write and tell us about yourself and what you can do. Make this summer one to remember – and get paid for it!

Write your **letter of application**. You should write between 120 and 180 words.

1 Should your writing be formal, semi-formal or informal? Why?
2 What information should you include?
3 Can you suggest any phrases that would be suitable for such a letter?
4 How can you start/end your letter?

24 **Read the model and answer the questions.**

Dear Sir or Madam,

1 With reference to your advertisement regarding the Westford Festival, I am writing to ask you to consider my application.

2 I am eighteen years old, female, and currently living in Munich, Germany. I will be in England for a year before I start university.

3 I enjoy looking after and organising activities for young children. Part of my work experience included working as a volunteer at a playgroup. Last year, I helped to organise our school sports day and I am sure this experience will be an advantage in planning events and exhibitions.

4 Please note that I am prepared to run errands, odd jobs and anything else you may consider that I am capable of. I have a good working knowledge of English and I consider myself to be both cheerful and energetic.

5 I will be arriving in June and can be contacted at the above address. Alternatively, my telephone number is 001 (0)344 8765432. Thank you for considering my application. I look forward to hearing from you soon.

Yours faithfully,

Suzanna Franke

Introduction

Paragraph 1

reason for writing

Main Body

Paragraphs 2-4

details of personal qualities / skills / abilities / experience etc

Conclusion

Final Paragraph

contact details / closing remarks

1 Where does the writer mention the reason for writing?
2 In which paragraph does the writer give details of her:
   a present situation
   b experience
   c willingness to work and personal qualities
   d contact details
3 Would you give Suzanna the job on the strength of this letter? Why (not)?
4 In pairs, think of an alternative beginning and ending for the letter.

Discuss and Write

25 Read the rubrics below, underline the key information and, for each one, answer the questions that follow.

A You recently entered a competition and have just received this letter from the organisers. Read the letter, together with the notes you have made on it. Then, using this information, write a suitable letter to the competition organisers.

Congratulations! You have won one of the top prizes in our competition – the latest model of the Flashtel mobile phone plus a free connection for six months.

In order to give you the phone and the connection which suits you best, we need to know the following:

About the phone itself:

- Colour preference (red, blue, green, yellow or black) ← Say which
- Do you want the phone to have an Internet connection or voice recognition? ← Internet, definitely

Do you expect to use your new mobile:

- during the day or in the evening? ← Tell them
- mostly for local or long-distance calls? ← Tell them
- from other countries? ← Mention the trip round Europe this summer

B You have been doing a class project on crime and your teacher has now asked you to write a composition about the following statement:
Crime is increasing – especially among young people.
Write your **composition**.

C A group of English students is planning to come to your town and the organisers have asked you for information on an important place of interest for them to visit. Write a report for the organisers, describing one place and giving reasons why you would recommend it for visitors.
Write your **report**.

D You see the following in an international magazine:

You are what you eat!

We are interested in readers' opinions on the subject of food and nutrition. Write us an article mentioning:

- what kinds of foods are popular with young people in your country
- what could be done to encourage healthy eating

The best articles will be published.

Write your **article**.

E You have decided to enter a short story competition. The rules of the competition state that your story must end with the following words:
With a huge smile on his face, Michael sat back and breathed a sigh of relief.
Write your **story**.

F You have just seen this advertisement in your local newspaper:

Wickering Summer Camp

We need young people to help out at this year's children's camp. The children are aged 8 - 14 and you will be required to:

- Help ensure the safety of the children
- Organise games and activities
- Help in the preparation of meals
- Do a variety of other important tasks

Think you can help us? Write and tell us about yourself and why you think you would be suitable for this job.

Write your **letter of application**.

1. What do you have to write?
2. What is your reason for writing?
3. Who is the target reader? What style is appropriate?
4. How many points must you include?
5. How will you arrange these points into paragraphs? Suggest how you could put them in your own words.
6. How could you begin and end your piece of writing?

26 Using the information you have learned, write TWO of the tasks you discussed above. You should write between 120 and 180 words for each one.

Appendix: Linking Words / Phrases

Personal opinion:	***In my opinion, / In my view, / To my mind, / To my way of thinking, / Personally I believe that / It strikes me that / I feel very strongly that / I am inclined to believe that / It seems to me that / As far as I am concerned, / I think that*** *the world would be a much better place without nuclear power.*
To list advantages and disadvantages:	***One advantage of / Another advantage of / One other advantage of / A further advantage of/The main advantage of / The greatest advantage of / The first advantage of*** *travelling to work by bicycle is that it is cheap; you don't have to pay for fuel.* ***One disadvantage of / Another disadvantage of / One other disadvantage of / A further disadvantage of / The main disadvantage of / The greatest disadvantage of / The first disadvantage of*** *travelling to work by bicycle is that you have no protection from the wind or rain.*
To list points:	***Firstly, / First of all, / In the first place, / Secondly, / Thirdly, / Finally, / To start with,*** *people who live in the country suffer far fewer health problems than those who live in the city.*
To list points in a specific sequence:	BEGINNING - ***First, / To start with, / To begin with,/ First of all,*** *wash the wound with cold water.* CONTINUING - ***Secondly, / After this/that, / Afterwards, / Then, / Next,*** *wrap a bandage around the cut.* CONCLUDING - ***Finally, / Lastly, / Last but not least,*** *place the patient in a comfortable position and allow them to rest.*
To add more points on the same topic:	***What is more, / Furthermore, / Apart from this/that, / In addition (to this), / Moreover, / Besides (this), / ... not to mention the fact that*** *cars are extremely expensive to maintain.* *Cars are* ***also*** *extremely expensive to maintain.* *Cars are extremely expensive to maintain* ***too.*** ***Not only*** *are cars harmful to the environment,* ***but*** *they are extremely expensive to maintain* ***as well.*** *Cars are* ***both*** *harmful to the environment* ***and*** *expensive to maintain.*
To refer to other sources:	***With reference to / According to*** *the article in yesterday's Guardian, the unemployment rate is falling in Britain.*
To express cause:	*The government decided not to fund the scheme* ***because /owing to the fact that / due to the fact that / on the grounds that / since / as*** *it seemed likely to fail.* ***In view of / Because of / Owing to*** *the scheme's high chances of failure, the government decided not to fund it.* *The scheme is likely to fail;* ***for this reason*** *the government has decided not to fund it.* ***Seeing that*** *the scheme is likely to fail, the government has decided not to fund it.* *The government has decided to fund the scheme* ***now that*** *its planners have redesigned it.*
To express effect:	*He passed his exams;* ***thus, / therefore, / so / consequently, / as a result, / as a consequence, / for this reason,*** *he was able to go to university.*
To express purpose:	*The government decided not to introduce the death penalty* ***for fear (that)*** *innocent people would die.* *The government decided not to introduce the death penalty* ***so that*** *innocent people would not die.* *The government decided not to introduce the death penalty* ***so as to / in order to*** *avoid the deaths of innocent people.* *The government decided not to introduce the death penalty* ***in case*** *it resulted in the death of innocent people.*

To emphasise what you say:	***Clearly, / Obviously, / Of course, / Needless to say,*** *if everyone were allowed to carry a gun, the crime rate would rise considerably.*
To express reality:	***It is a fact that / In effect, / In fact, / As a matter of fact, / The fact of the matter is (that) / Actually, / In practice, / Indeed, / To tell you the truth,*** *a crash helmet would be quite useless in the event of a serious motorcycle accident.*
To express the difference between appearance and reality:	***Initially, / At first, / At first sight,*** *his injuries seemed minor, but when the doctors examined him, they discovered he had fractured his skull.*
To give examples:	***For instance, / For example,*** *by reducing your intake of red meat you can decrease your chances of having a heart attack in later life.* *By reducing your intake of foods* ***such as / like*** *beef and lamb you can decrease your chances of having a heart attack in later life.* *If you want to decrease your chances of having a heart attack in later life, you should reduce your intake of meat,* ***particularly / in particular, / especially*** *red meat.*
To make general statements:	***As a general rule, / Generally, / In general, / On the whole,*** *people who exercise regularly suffer fewer stress-related problems than those who don't.*
To make partially correct statements:	***Up to a point, / To a certain extent, / To some extent, / In a sense, / In a way,*** *this is true as women in society are far less likely to use physical violence than men.*
To express limit of knowledge:	***To the best of my knowledge, / As far as I know,*** *there is no firm proof of the existence of aliens.*
To state other people's opinion:	***It is popularly believed that / People often claim that / It is often alleged that / Some people argue that / Many argue that / A lot of people think that / A lot of people believe that*** *the earth is the only planet in our solar system that has ever supported life.* ***Contrary to popular belief,*** *the earth is not the only planet in our solar system to have supported life.*
To make contrasting points:	*It is a known fact that smoking causes cancer,* ***yet / however, / nevertheless, / but / at the same time / even so, / still, / nonetheless,*** *millions of people around the world continue to smoke.* ***Although / Even though / Regardless of the fact that / In spite of the fact that / Despite the fact that / While*** *it is a known fact that smoking causes cancer, millions of people around the world continue to smoke.*
To express balance (the other side of the argument):	*Dogs are good pets in that they provide companionship;* ***however, / but / on the other hand, / although / yet, / at the same time, / in contrast,*** *feeding and grooming a dog can be expensive and time-consuming.*
Negative addition:	***Neither*** *the prime minister* ***nor*** *his deputy knew anything about the experiment.* ***Neither*** *of them knew anything about the experiment.* *The prime minister didn't know anything about the experiment;* ***nor / neither*** *did his deputy.* *The prime minister didn't know anything about the experiment and his deputy didn't* ***either.***
To express exception:	*He read all the books* ***but/apart from/except (for)*** *one: "Oliver Twist".*
To clarify/rephrase:	***In other words,/That is to say,/To put it another way,*** *if people made more of an effort to protect the environment, the world would be a much healthier place to live in.*

To express similarity:	*Alcohol reduces our ability to concentrate on our work;* ***similarly,/likewise,/in the same way,*** *it reduces our ability to concentrate while driving.*
To give an alternative:	*We could switch to* ***(either)*** *solar power* ***or*** *wind power.* *We could switch to solar power.* ***On the other hand,/Alternatively,*** *wind power is also an environmentally friendly option.*
To express condition:	*I told him that he could borrow my car* ***on the condition that / provided (that) / providing (that) / only if / as long as*** *he didn't drive it too fast.* ***In the event of*** *trouble, /* ***In the event that*** *trouble should start, /* ***If*** *trouble should start, lock all the doors and windows.* *Take an umbrella* ***in case of*** *rain/****in case*** *it rains.* *He asked me* ***whether (or not)*** *I wanted to go.* *You had better lock all the doors* ***otherwise/or (else)*** *you will be in trouble.*
To express the consequence of a condition:	*The company is hoping for a government loan;* ***consequently,/then/so/in which case,*** *it will be able to provide fifty new jobs.* *I'm hoping the club will be open tonight;* ***if so,*** *we'll have a great time,* ***if not,/otherwise,*** *we'll have to go home.*
To express comparison:	*This car is* ***as*** *fast* ***as / more*** *comfortable* ***than / twice as*** *fast* ***as / less*** *comfortable* ***than*** *mine.*
To conclude:	***Finally,/Lastly,/Above all,/All in all,/Taking everything into account,/On the whole,/All things considered,/In conclusion,/As I have said,/As was previously stated,/To sum up,*** *it is unlikely that mankind will ever bring an end to all wars.*
Time:	*Press the button* ***when/whenever/before/until/till/after*** *the light comes on.* *I haven't seen him* ***since*** *June.* *I saw him* ***as*** *I was leaving the shop./ I saw him* ***while*** *I was doing my shopping.* *I never see him* ***now that*** *he lives in Canada.*
Relatives:	*That's the man* ***who/that*** *gave me the bag.* *That's the man* ***whose*** *bag it is.* *That's the dog* ***which/that*** *bit me.* *That's the place* ***where*** *I live.* *That's the woman* ***who/whom/that*** *I live with.*
Reference:	*I wish to make a complaint* ***regarding/concerning*** *one of your shop assistants.* *I am writing* ***with respect/regard/reference to / in regard/reference to*** *your recent letter of application.*
Summarising:	***In short/Briefly/To put it briefly,*** *the film was the best I've ever seen.*